"This is the way the world ends
This is the way the world ends
This is the way the world ends
Not with a bang but a whimper."
—T. S. Eliot

"His dominion is an everlasting dominion
Which will not pass away;
And His kingdom is one
Which will not be destroyed."
—Daniel 7:14

Two mortal men peering into the future—but what a contrast! Using the eye of faith, God's prophets have left us a breathtaking view of history ahead—a view that both calms our fears and challenges our priorities and life-styles.

In this survey, Dr. Larry Richards introduces us to visionary leaders such as Ezra and Nehemiah... and mind-stretching seers such as Daniel, Zechariah, Haggai, and Zephaniah. The concluding chapters are a sweeping synthesis of the Old Testament portrait of destiny.

Other BIBLE ALIVE titles:

OLD TESTAMENT SURVEYS

Let Day Begin
Freedom Road
Years of Darkness, Days of Glory
Edge of Judgment
Lift High the Torch

NEW TESTAMENT SURVEYS

The Servant King
The Great Adventure
Regions Beyond
Christ Preeminent
Pass It On
His Glory

LARRY RICHARDS
BIBLE ALIVE SERIES

Springtime Coming

Prophetic Themes of the Old Testament

Studies in Ezra, Nehemiah, Esther, Daniel, Zephaniah, Haggai, Zechariah, and Malachi

David C. Cook Publishing Co.
ELGIN, ILLINOIS—WESTON, ONTARIO

SPRINGTIME COMING

Old Testament quotations, unless noted otherwise, are from the New American Standard Bible, © The Lockman Foundation 1960, 1962, 1963, 1968, 1971, and are used by permission. New Testament quotations, unless noted otherwise, are from the New International Version.

Street map on page 29 courtesy of Zondervan Publishing House. Reproduced from Vol. 1, *Zondervan Pictorial Bible Encyclopedia* © 1975 by The Zondervan Corporation. Used by permission.

Published by David C. Cook Publishing Co.
850 N. Grove Ave., Elgin, IL 60120
Edited by Dean Merrill
Cover photo by Ed Elsner
Printed in the United States of America

ISBN 0-89191-094-8
LC 77-78504

CONTENTS

Part One
THE EXILES RETURN

1

Ezra 1–6; Haggai

LOOK HOMEWARD

IT WAS 538 B.C.

And it felt like springtime.

I remember one Christmas when it felt like springtime to me. I'd been working on the *Harrisburg* (Pa.) *Evening News* for four months. I wanted to go home to Michigan for the holidays but didn't have train fare.

Then it came. Just a few dollars, but enough. When I realized I could go home after all, even the brutal Pennsylvania cold seemed warm. There was a fresh stirring of life, not in nature, but in me! I was going home! I could feel springtime coming.

That's what it was like in 538 for the Jewish captives in Babylon. Hope was reborn. They looked toward their far-off land with new urgency. As travel plans were made and permissions were granted, fresh life stirred deep within.

WINTER

In our previous book *Edge of Judgment,* we traced Israel's gradual turning away from her God. Apostasy gathered increasing momentum until the whole nation was in a headlong rush toward judgment.

The Jews had been content with idolatry and injustice, lulled by material prosperity into a false sense of well-being. As long as the food was rich, the wines plentiful, and the houses comfortable, nothing else seemed to matter. Israel had given itself to pleasure and found a fleshly excitement in the sensual excesses of pagan worship that made the austere joys of holiness seem empty by comparison. Somehow relationship with God, a sense of call as His Chosen People, a commitment to holiness and justice, a love for other people—all these seemed unimportant. Like Esau, the Jews of the surviving kingdom (722-586 B.C.) had finally come to the place where they were quick to trade their birthright for a bowl of soup.

Then God brought the Babylonian armies down on His people. The land was crushed by the military might of Nebuchadnezzar; the luxuries were stripped away. Beginning with the upper classes, the Jewish people were led away captive. With pride ground into the dirt, men and women stumbled along on foot behind their captors. The humiliation of Israel was complete.

Through humiliation, Israel began to learn. In Babylon the Jews were well treated. They had their own homes. They had their own elders and retained their customs. They went into business, and many prospered. The luxuries they had lived for in Palestine were in Babylon too. But for many Jews, it wasn't the same. A deep longing grew for the land they had left, for the worship of Jehovah they had discounted, and for that distinctive way of life under His Law that they had ignored. They suddenly realized that the intangible things were in fact the values on which life must be based. The material and tangible things they had once valued were empty indeed.

In the poetry of Lamentations, you can hear the longing of the captives and sense the winter in their souls.

How lonely sits the city
That was full of people!
She has become like a widow
Who was once great among the nations!
She who was a princess among the provinces
Has become a forced laborer! . . .
In the days of her affliction and homelessness
Jerusalem remembers all her precious things
That were from the days of old. . . .
"Is it nothing to all you who pass this way?
Look and see if there is any pain like my pain
Which was severely dealt out to me,
Which the Lord inflicted on the day of His fierce
anger. . . ."

Remember, O Lord, what has befallen us;
Look, and see our reproach!

Our inheritance has been turned over to strangers,
Our houses to aliens.
We have become orphans without a father,
Our mothers are like widows.
We have to pay for our drinking water,
Our wood comes to us at a price.
Our pursuers are at our necks;
We are worn out, there is no rest for us.
We have submitted to Egypt and Assyria to get enough bread.
Our fathers sinned, and are no more;
It is we who have borne their iniquities. . . .
Elders are gone from the gate,
Young men from their music.
The joy of our hearts has ceased;
Our dancing has been turned to mourning.
The crown has fallen from our head;
Woe to us, for we have sinned!
Because of this our heart is faint;
Because of these things our eyes are dim;
Because of Mount Zion which lies desolate,
Foxes prowl in it.

Lamentations 1:1, 7, 12 and 5:1-7, 14-18

In spite of increasingly improved conditions in Babylon, Israel could not wipe away the picture of her humiliation. The songs of Lamentations were constant reminders that

the worldly thing men
set their hearts upon turns ashes

or it flourishes, and soon
like snow upon the desert's dusty face
is gone.[1]

In the winter of the Captivity, Israel's misery drove her to a new turning. Men pored over the writings of the prophets and of Moses to understand what had happened. Out of this return to the Word of God grew the synagogue, the local gathering place for the Jews. New hope was born.

STIRRINGS OF SPRING

There were a number of sources of the rebirth of hope. The prophets Jeremiah and Ezekiel, contemporary to the Exile, not only warned of judgment but spoke of the faithfulness of God to His Covenant promises. God would return them to the Promised Land (Jer. 31); His Covenant with Abraham would be kept; the Temple would be rebuilt (Ezek. 40f).

Jeremiah's writings had indicated that the Captivity would last only for some seventy years (Jer. 25:11-21; 29:10). Over a century and a half before, God had even given through Isaiah the very name of the ruler who would accomplish the return:

"It is I who says of Cyrus, 'He is My shepherd!
And he will perform all My desire.'
And he declares of Jerusalem, 'She will be built,'
And of the temple, 'Your foundation will be laid.' "

Isaiah 44:28

And God had again spoken through Isaiah about this pagan ruler as His own anointed.

> "I have aroused him in righteousness
> And I will make all his ways smooth;
> He will build My city, and will let My exiles go free,
> Without any payment or reward," says the Lord of hosts.
>
> *Isaiah 45:13*

You can imagine the excitement in the Hebrew community in Babylon as word of a Persian conqueror named Cyrus drifted into the capital. By 550 B.C. Cyrus had formed a large domain known in history as Media-Persia. Bent on world conquest, Cyrus now defeated Babylon's ally Croesus and in 539 B.C. took Babylon itself without a fight. There, in October of 539, Cyrus was welcomed by the people of Babylon as a liberator and accomplished an amazingly easy transfer of power. Truly God had made "all his ways smooth"!

Then, in the first year of his rule, Cyrus announced a startling reversal of the Babylonian resettlement policy. We have portions of his decree recorded in our Bibles.

> "Thus says Cyrus king of Persia, 'The Lord, the God of heaven, has given me all the kingdoms of the earth, and He has appointed me to build Him a house in Jerusalem, which is in Judah. Whoever there is among you of all His people, may his God be with Him! Let him go up to Jerusalem which is

> in Judah, and rebuild the house of the Lord, the God of Israel; He is the God who is in Jerusalem. And every survivor, at whatever place he may live, let the men of that place support him with silver and gold, with goods and cattle, together with a freewill offering for the house of God which is in Jerusalem."
>
> *Ezra 1:2-4*

Springtime had come.
The Jewish people were going home!

THE RETURN

Ezra 1-3

Not everyone was eager to return.

While many had reexamined their values and commitments, a great number of those who prospered in Babylon were again enmeshed in materialism. In fact, the report of Ezra makes it clear that those who did return were especially those "whose spirit God had stirred to go up and rebuild the house of the Lord" (1:5). They did receive enthusiastic support from the rest of the Jewish community. They were given gold, silver, and beasts of burden; in addition, all the treasures of the first Temple that had been carried off to Babylon were now returned by Cyrus (1:6-11). So the 42,360 Israelites—plus their 7,337 servants!—did not return as paupers. They were well equipped to rebuild the Temple and to reestablish Jerusalem as a significant city.

Ezra, who tells us about this springtime pilgrimage of 538 B.C., was not among the rejoicing company. He had not yet been born . . . but some eighty years later, Ezra would lead another company along the highway home. The leader of this first group was a man called Zerubbabel (his Hebrew name) or Sheshbazzar (his Chaldean name; see Ezra 3:8; 5:16; Zech. 4:9). He and the high priest Joshua guided the people back to their homeland and, once there, quickly began work on the Temple. First, though, they erected an altar and reinstated the sacrifices God had prescribed through Moses. They also kept the commanded Feast of Tabernacles.

In May they began to lay the foundation of the new Temple. As soon as it was finished, they called all the people together to celebrate. The Bible tells us that "they sang praising and giving thanks to the Lord, saying, 'For He is good, for His lovingkindness is upon Israel forever' " (Ezra 3:11).

The shouts of joy were mixed with tears as the older men who could remember the glory of Solomon's Temple compared its magnificence with the more modest dimensions of the new. But the shouts of joy and tears could not really be distinguished; the shout of celebration was so great only its triumph could be heard.

What mattered was not the size.

What mattered was that once again a Temple to God was being built.

The Temple. Why was the Temple so important to the Jews? What was the significance of its rebuilding?

In the ancient world, deities were associated with particular locations, viewed either as the home or a favorite haunt of the god. Thus temples were constructed as residences for the god or goddess manifested there, and it was assumed that the deities found these residences acceptable. No wonder Cyrus referred to Jehovah as "the God who is in Jerusalem" (1:3).

This way of thinking did *not* underlie the significance of the Temple in Israel. As Solomon asked in his prayer of dedication, "Will God indeed dwell on the earth? Behold, heaven and the highest heaven cannot contain Thee, how much less this house which I have built!" (1 Kings 8:27).

Still God did promise Israel that in a special sense He would focus His presence with them through the Temple. Even as early as Moses' day, God indicated that one day the Lord would choose a place "to make his name dwell there," and that that place was to be the only location for offering sacrifices (Deut. 12:11). The central place of worship would be a unique unifying force for Israel. Three times a year the Jews were to gather from throughout their land to worship there, reaffirming their common faith and common heritage as God's Covenant people.

By limiting the sacrifices to this one location, Israel was also to be protected from the pattern of pagan worship common in the Near East, according to which gods and goddesses were worshiped in many localities—high hills, sacred groves, secluded caves. The single place of worship set aside to meet Jehovah was thus a unique affirmation of the oneness of God and of the commitment Israel was to maintain to Him and to Him alone. In the words of Moses, chanted in every synagogue even today, "Hear, O Israel! The Lord is our God, the Lord is one! And you shall love the Lord your God with all your heart and with all your soul and with all your might" (Deut. 6:4). In the heart of the believer, as in the public worship of Israel, there was to be room only for One.

But the significance of the Temple is not fully seen even in this great distinctive. There was as well a great portrait of God's plan in the Temple design. As in the Tabernacle (which we studied in the second Old Testament book of the **Bible Alive** series, *Freedom Road),* the pattern given by God spoke of access into God's presence through the blood of sacrifice. The design also spoke of worship, divine guidance, and supernatural supply. In the pattern of the building and its courts the believing Jew could see reflected realities of his relationship with God.

These important roles of the Temple in the faith of the Old Testament would be enough to explain the drive to rebuild that motivated the thousands who enthusiastically left Babylon and headed home. But as we read more deeply in Ezra, and particularly hear the message of the prophet Haggai, there was a deeper reason yet.

GOOD INTENTIONS

Ezra 4-6; Haggai 1:1–2:19

The foundation of the Temple was laid in 537 B.C.

in the flush of quickened enthusiasm.

But almost immediately, opposition was stirred. The peoples who had been imported into Palestine by Nebuchadnezzar had settled down in Israel and Judah. The new settlers had carried over much of old religions . . . but they also adopted the God of the new land! They did not know Him personally. They were not His Covenant people. But it was only safe, after all, to acknowledge and worship Him along with the others.

Thus when whe Jews returned to rebuild the Temple, these foreigners requested, "Let us build with you; for we, like you, seek your God; and we have been sacrificing to Him since the days of Esarhaddon king of Assyria, who brought us up here" (4:2).

This request was denied flatly: "You have nothing in common with us," Zerubbabel and Jeshua and the other leaders replied (4:3). These people were not of Abraham's line. They were not children of the Covenant. And they were to have no part of a ministry God had committed to His own and only to His own.

This blunt reply angered the Samaritans (a name for these strangers that carried on into and beyond New Testament times). They immediately began to oppose the Jews, even sending paid lobbyists to government centers (Ezra 4:5) to block further work on the Temple. They were so successful that for some sixteen years the Temple remained little more than a bare foundation.

During these years, the people built homes for

themselves. They planted fields and laid out vineyards. Apparently they spent much of the fund committed to them for building the Temple. Yet, in spite of their efforts, they did not prosper. They had permitted opposition to turn them from their commitment to God, and the springtime in their heart had withered away.

Then, on September 1, 520 B.C., the prophet Haggai recalled them to the task with these jolting words:

> "Thus says the Lord of hosts, 'This people says, "The time has not come, even the time for the house of the Lord to be rebuilt." ' . . . Is it time for you yourselves to dwell in your paneled houses while this house lies desolate?" Now therefore, thus says the Lord of hosts, "Consider your ways! You have sown much, but harvest little; you eat, but there is not enough to be satisfied; you drink, but there is not enough to become drunk; you put on clothing, but no one is warm enough; and he who earns, earns wages to put into a purse with holes. . . . Why?" declares the Lord of hosts, "Because of My house which lies desolate, while each of you runs to his own house."
>
> *Haggai 1:2, 4-6, 9*

That first flush of commitment to God had been dissipated by their difficulties, and in their daily efforts to meet their material needs they had forgotten to make God the center of their lives. "You shall love the Lord your God with all your heart, and with

HAGGAI'S FOUR MESSAGES (520 B.C.)	
1:1-15	Sept. 1
2:1-9	Oct. 21
2:10-19	Dec. 24
2:20-23	Dec. 24

all your soul, and with all your might," echoed the ancient words of Deuteronomy (6:4). The timelessness of this call to make God the focus and center of the believer's life is reflected further in Jesus' New Testament words, "Seek ye first the kingdom of God, and his righteousness; and all these things shall be added unto you" (Matt. 6:33, KJV).

In a series of jolting exhortations Haggai, joined by Zechariah, stirred the people of Israel to action. Once again Zerubbabel and Jeshua led the people to build, the opposition of the Samaritans was overcome (Ezra 5-6), and in four years the restored Temple stood on the site of the first, which had been destroyed in 586.

It was 516 B.C.

The seventy years foretold by Jeremiah were past. With the Temple restored, Israel was once again officially in the promised land.

THE BREATH OF SPRING
Haggai 2:20-23

In reading the message of Haggai, we might get the mistaken impression that the primary motivation to resume work on the Temple was materialistic—the promise of blessing.

If so, we would be misreading the motivation that brought these pilgrims back to the land of Palestine. To the Jews of the return, Palestine was a frontier. The devastation of conquest had scarred the Promised Land; the fertile fields were seared, the vines uprooted, the olive trees shattered. These men and women had in fact made very great material sacrifices to leave the civilization and comfort of Babylon to risk their futures in an attempt to recover their past. Many Jews had been unwilling to make this kind of sacrifice.

The opposition of the Samaritans had stunned them. The difficulties of life in Palestine had worn them down. It is true that the exiles had lost that early sense of commitment under the grinding pressures of rebuilding their lives in the shattered land. But these were men and women whose hearts God had stirred (Ezra 1:5). As the prophet cried out to them now, their hearts were stirred again.

Difficulties were seen in a fresh perspective and recognized as a natural outcome of their failure to put God first. Blessing would follow their return to commitment. But they would return for God's sake—not for the sake of the blessing.

It is the final message of Haggai that makes this all clear. A final message, because beyond this exciting promise the prophet had no need to go. "I am going to shake the heavens and the earth. And I will overthrow the thrones of kingdoms," the Lord said through Haggai (2:21-22). *The shaking of the nations was drawing near.* The Messiah would one day come. When He appeared, He would want to stand in the

Temple, for it would become "the place of My throne and the place of the soles of My feet, where I will dwell among the sons of Israel forever" (Ezek. 43:7).

Haggai's message served to pull the attention of Israel away from their present and direct their eyes once again to the future. For the destiny of Israel, as the destiny of believers today, *did* lie in the future. Hearing the prophet's words, looking beyond the present, the people of God could see the shadowy form of the divine deliverance. They could hear the distant echoes of His victory cries. They could sense the very ground quiver beneath their feet. Somehow, once again the future seemed more real than the now. Stirred, the Temple was rebuilt because a new sense of springtime had replaced the winter in their hearts.

GOING DEEPER

These study suggestions will guide your reading of the Bible portions introduced in the chapters of this book. They will help you examine the message of each passage—and help you think of its personal meaning to you.

to personalize

1. Several passages will give you the feel of this important period of Bible history. Look at each, and jot down anything you observe in a quick scanning.

- Lamentations 1, 5 (the feeling of captivity)
- Ezra 1—4 (motives for the return)

- Ezra 5—6 (the fresh start)

2. Haggai is a small but interesting book. It records a series of short sermons or exhortations and tells of the people's response. What is striking is that this generation, unlike their fathers, did respond and obey the words of the prophet. Using the outline given on page 21, study this little book carefully. What was the thrust of each message? How did the hearers respond? How do you account for their response?

3. In *Springtime Coming* we will be looking at the impact of prophecy (as a foretelling of the future) on the lives of God's people. How would you describe the probable impact on the people of Judah of (1) Isaiah's prophecy about Cyrus (see pp. 13-14) and (2) Haggai's prophecy about the shaking of the nations.

4. Can you think of prophecies that have had an impact on your own life? Jot down what they are, and explain briefly their impact.

5. Think for a moment. If you knew what the future holds, how would that affect your attitude toward the present? Why?

1. *The Rubaiyat of Omar Khayyam.*

2

historical survey; Esther

FROM THE ASHES

THE BABYLONIAN CAPTIVITY had been intensely painful. Yet the prophets of earlier days had promised that when God ripped His people from their land, He would restore them. Restoration would prove His continuing love.

Looking back, it's clear that the Captivity had many positive outcomes. In Ezra's story of the first company's return, we read of a fresh responsiveness to God and an obedience to the word of His prophets that is uncharacteristic of preceding generations. The impact of the Exile was so great that it affected the life-style and commitment of the Jewish people long beyond New Testament times. This is seen not only in the institution of the synagogue, but in a new focus on Scripture. A. C. Schultz summarizes:

> Among the results of the Exile for Israel was a more profound comprehension of the law of Moses and the

> prophets as important for the Jews as a people. There came also a clearer grasp of the universality and sovereignty of God; that Yahweh is one and there is no god beside Him. This faith remained so unshakable that it withstood the influence and fascination of Greek culture in spite of Hellenism's effects upon some other areas of Judaism and the rest of the Mediterranean world.[1]

And the Captivity did something else. It helped to weaken the Israelites' fatal fascination with the material comforts to be gained in the present. It reaffirmed the fact that just as their identity was rooted in the past, their destiny was waiting in the future.

IDENTITY AND DESTINY

For Israel, *identity* was firmly rooted in history. The nation and the individual were Covenant people, recipients through birth and faith of the great promises God had made long ago to Abraham and confirmed to Abraham's children. As a special people, Israel had been given the divine law, which explained how they were to live to glorify God and to experience blessings in each new generation.

But for Israel, *destiny* could never again be summed up as prosperity. No, destiny also was firmly rooted . . . in history to come! The whole tenor of the prophets' messages to Israel, the whole thrust of the initial Covenant strains forward in time toward a coming fulfillment. One day soon, the nations will be shaken. One day soon, the Messiah will come. One day soon, Israel will take her promised place as queen of the nations.

For the men and women who returned to rebuild the Temple in Jerusalem, it was this hope, springing from the ashes of Palestine's now-barren land, that began to grow and to bud like a young plant. The Jews looked forward to their destiny . . . and the vision of destiny brought the springtime.

RECOVERY OF SPRING

In a way, we can look at this period of Bible history as a time when Israel recovered both something of her sense of identity and her sense of destiny.

The days of the Captivity and the following return are complex, and it is important before we go into the writings of the period to have an overview of the events.

Defeat. The Captivity involved a series of invasions by Babylonian armies, a series of submissions by Judah and deportations of groups of Jews, a series of rebellions against Babylonian garrisons, and ultimately the complete destruction of Jerusalem and the Temple, followed by the flight by the last remnant of Israelites toward Egypt.

During the times of defeat, God had spoken to His people through two major prophets. Jeremiah, who was with the people in Judah, had constantly urged surrender to Babylon and acceptance of God's ordained judgment. He was severely persecuted for this "unpatriotic" message, and the Word of the Lord through him was rejected or ignored. The

Book of Jeremiah records the messages of this "weeping prophet" and sketches the situation in Judah during the last years of the surviving kingdom.

Ezekiel, a young man who had been deported with an early group of captives, prophesied to the Jews in Babylon. He confirmed the messages of Jeremiah concerning the coming judgment, and while he had considerable influence, his warnings were also ignored until the destruction finally occurred in 586.

The messages of both Jeremiah and Ezekiel focused on warnings. Yet often each shifted to speak of the more distant future with words of hope. Jeremiah spoke of a New Covenant that God would one day make with His people: a Covenant through which He would give them new hearts, and take the Law that had been written on stone tablets and write it again on their living personalities. The people of Israel had ignored the external Law; when the Law was written *within* them, God's people would at last be responsive to Him.

Ezekiel's vision of the future is a vision of peace. He speaks of a time when the worship of God is universal not only in Israel but in all the world. In the last chapters of his book, Ezekiel sketches a great temple to be constructed in the days of Israel's destiny and outlines the blessings that God's presence will bring to His people.

In Babylon. Another of the early captives taken to Babylon was the young Daniel. Trained for Nebuchadnezzar's civil service, he advanced quickly

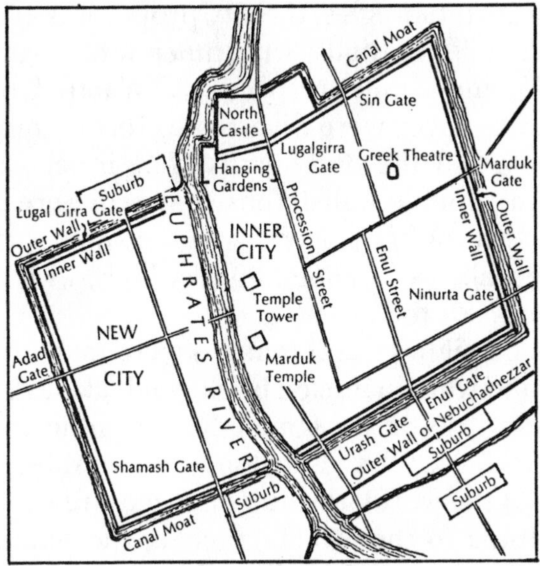

THE CITY OF BABYLON

and played significant roles in the administration of several great kings.

But he was also given specific prophetic revelations dealing with the days of Gentile dominion—those centuries during which the Jews would be subservient to a succession of Gentile world powers. Daniel also was given amazingly specific prophecies concerning the coming of the Messiah—the Anointed One whom God would appoint to lead Israel to her destiny.

For a person living in ancient Babylon, the vision of Israel's destiny would have been particularly vital. Babylon was the capital of a vast empire and was itself unbelievably impressive. Laid out carefully with broad paved avenues running parallel or intersecting at right angles, the city proper was enclosed with 42 miles of walls, with inner walls extending 2½, 4½, and 7 miles respectively. Waters from the Euphrates River were diverted to form a moat defense around the outer walls. The inner walls of Babylon's double-wall defensive system were 21 feet thick, with towers placed at 60-foot intervals. The middle walls were some 300 feet high, with towers reaching 420 feet.

Public buildings and temples were magnificently decorated with enameled brick, gold, alabaster, and striking works of art. Under Nebuchadnezzar, and later under Cyrus, Babylon was considered the center of the world, the hub of an empire stretching from India to the Mediterranean, the pinnacle of military and administrative achievement.

For the deported Israelites, many of whom were at first put to work as artisans in the massive building programs undertaken to further beautify the capital city, the power of this great world empire must have seemed far more real than the prophet's dreams of future glory. And yet, as the Chosen People turned back to the Book of God . . . and as Daniel knelt in prayer to receive God's revelations . . . a fresh awareness of reality began to grow. Somehow the unseen took on a firmness and solidarity no longer retained by the things that could be touched and felt. The desire grew to return to the land of promise. To wait. To wait for Israel's destiny.

The Jewish queen. In the meantime, significant contingents of Jews spread out to form Hebrew communities in other commercial centers throughout the empire. These Jews enjoyed the freedom to live and work and move about.

The most vivid incident dealing with these Jews is related in the Book of Esther. This book tells of Esther winning the position of queen in her marriage to Xerxes, of the subsequent attack on the Jews by a high court official, and of God's use of Queen Esther to turn aside the blow. Here in this book of the Bible God's name is not mentioned—yet His sovereign and providential care for Israel behind the scenes is clear.

Esther's husband, incidentally, was the same Xerxes who was thrown back in his attempt to destroy the Greeks at the Battle of Salamis.

In the land. Meanwhile, back in Judea, the returnees completed the Temple, listened to the words of the prophets Haggai and Zechariah, and settled down to await Messiah. But in the wait, their hearts again began to drift from God and thoughts of His springtime. Ezra's return in 458 B.C. recalled them to the Law. Nehemiah in 445 purified a people who had again fallen into disobedience and, by his vigorous leadership, moved them to rebuild the walls of Jerusalem. But when Nehemiah returned for a time to Babylon, the people quickly drifted again into their old habits of disobedience and self-will. Finally Malachi, the last of the Old Testament prophets, spoke out in a series of searing questions that reveal how far God's people had drifted from awareness of their destiny.

And yet . . .

And yet the writings of these post-exilic prophets

are as full of warning and hope as were the words of the former prophets. These spokesmen for God continued to call His people to Him—and continued to sketch a picture of Israel's destiny that even now captures our imagination and awakens in our own hearts a yearning for the future God has in store for Planet Earth.

When we catch a vision of that future, we too are caught up in an awareness of destiny that can change our attitudes, reshape our values, vitalize our faith, and give birth to springtime in our own hearts. And it is this vision—this journey into springtime—that we are concerned about in this book of the **Bible Alive Series.** For God *has* spoken through His prophets. In their words we find a picture of the future that helps us realize what the joyful company of returning Jews had finally grasped.

The glory that was Babylon would one day fall into ruins—and it has. The glories of our modern world, the splendor of our accomplishments, await that same decay. But when Messiah comes . . . ! Then we will meet our destiny. And to *that* kingdom there shall be no end.

GOING DEEPER

to personalize

1. You'll want to familiarize yourself with the history of this period, so that you can fit the Bible passages we'll read into its framework. First look over the chart on pages 178-79, and if this study is

part of a credit course, memorize the bold face (darker) section. Then study the time line on page 34 until you get the sequence and relationship of events clearly in mind.

2. Two passages of Scripture make fascinating reading to catch the flavor of this period. Read each quickly, for enjoyment.

- 2 Chronicles 36 (the background of judgment)
- Esther (God's providential care)

3. Go back and reread Esther once again. Note particularly (1) evidences of God's care for His people; (2) evidences of God's supervision of history.

4. Often God's workings in history are hidden, in that He seems to work through "natural" causes rather than miracles. Can you see in Esther any principles of His workings that might help you explain (or develop!) your own confidence that God is at work in hidden ways in your own life?

5. The author suggests that a sense of destiny (as well as a sense of identity) is vital for the believer. From the outline of history in this chapter, what *specific values* of a sense of destiny can you see for Israel?

6. What is your understanding of your destiny as a Christian? See how many different helpful values you can list for maintaining a sense of destiny.

to probe

1. Find out all you can about the city of Babylon in the days of Nebuchadnezzar and/or Cyrus.

2. Read one or two other sources to get a more

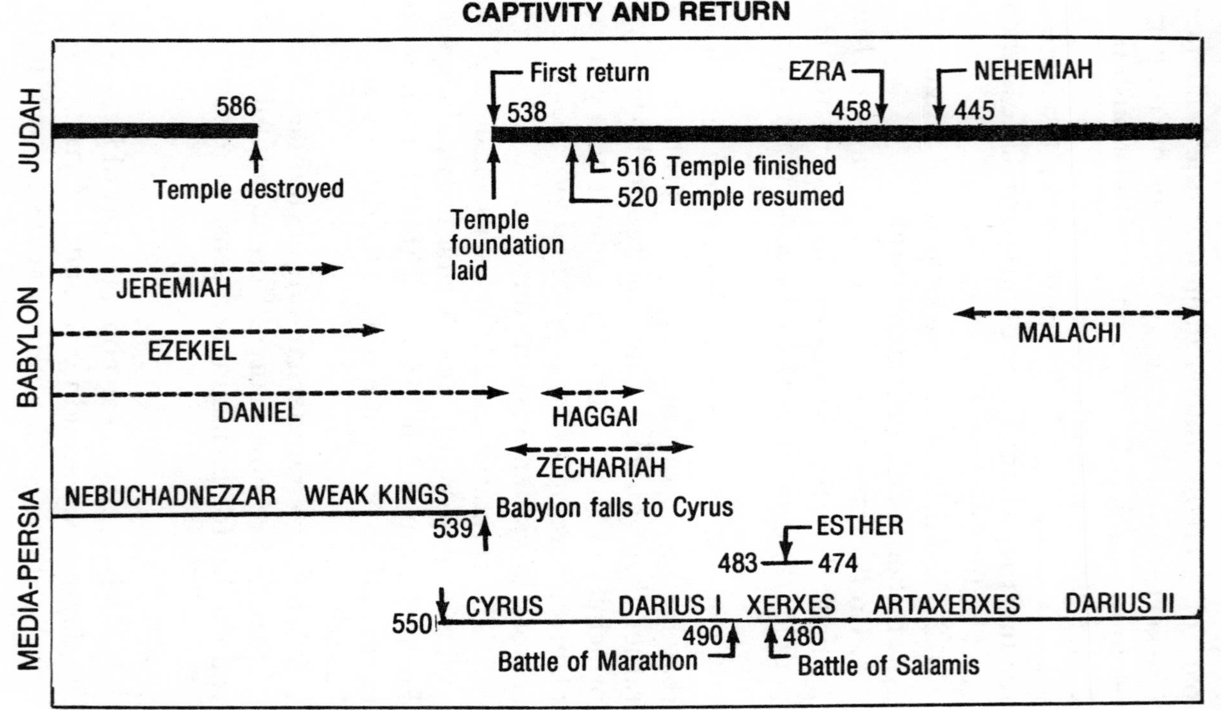
CAPTIVITY AND RETURN
JUDAH
586
Temple destroyed
First return
538
Temple foundation laid
516 Temple finished
520 Temple resumed
EZRA
458
NEHEMIAH
445
BABYLON
JEREMIAH
EZEKIEL
DANIEL
HAGGAI
ZECHARIAH
MALACHI
MEDIA-PERSIA
NEBUCHADNEZZAR
WEAK KINGS
539
Babylon falls to Cyrus
ESTHER
483
474
550
CYRUS
DARIUS I
XERXES
ARTAXERXES
DARIUS II
490
Battle of Marathon
480
Battle of Salamis

detailed picture of the time of the Captivity and return.

3. Research several sources to discover the lasting impacts of the Captivity on Israel. It's clear that they did not retain the sense of springtime that motivated their return and rebuilding of the Temple. What did they retain? What institutions, practices, and ideas stem from this period? Write a three- to four-page report on your findings.

1. *Zondervan Pictorial Encyclopedia of the Bible* (Grand Rapids: Zondervan, 1974) 1:428.

3

Ezra 7-10; Nehemiah

NEW BEGINNINGS

HOLLIS WAS A GOOD MAN: a sincere Christian, well liked by everyone who knew him. Yet whenever there was an altar call in the church he attended—an invitation to those who felt a need to rededicate themselves to the Lord—Hollis was always the first to respond.

It was hard to understand why. One of his sons was a friend of mine; in the time I spent in his home I saw no evidence of faults or failings. My parents were sure that Hollis was the last man in that congregation who needed rededication. Yet in his heart Hollis must have felt a need for new beginnings and must have seen each altar call as an opportunity for a fresh start.

As an adult, I've yearned many times for a fresh start myself. Not that my spiritual commitment or relationship has changed. But somehow, many little things get warped and twisted—habits develop, ways of thinking and feeling and responding intrude that do not fit with what I want to be. I'd like to wipe them all out and start again, with a sense of freshness and restoration. I'd like to make a new beginning.

I suspect that the desire for a fresh start is something each of us experiences. Guilt feelings are often the source of our sense of need.

Somehow we feel that if we had *really* committed ourselves to God that last time, we'd not need a fresh start now. Our life would be one consistent experience of victory, one steady journey on an upward path. It's painful to discover that even after sincere dedication, we can fall. Somehow our hearts tend to drift, until we're jolted into awareness that we need yet another new beginning.

It was a jolt for men like Ezra and Nehemiah to discover that Israel needed fresh starts. The people of God had returned to the land with great expectations; they enthusiastically journeyed hundreds of miles to rebuild the Temple . . . and stopped with the bare foundations. Stirred up by Haggai and Zechariah, they made a fresh beginning and completed the Temple in expectation of Messiah. But years passed. He did not come. And the old patterns of life, the old materialism, the old values, crept in.

There was no excuse.

It was wrong.

But it happened to them . . . just as it happens to you and me. When a people or an individual does drift from God, it's time for recommitment. Time for the fresh start God is always willing to give us when we turn to Him.

EZRA

In the seventh year of Artaxerxes Longimanus, 458 B.C., just fifty-eight years after the completion of the Temple, Ezra led a group of some fifteen hundred men and their families back to Palestine.

In Ezra's day, Palestine was part of a larger governmental unit, the satrapy of Abarnahara, and was ruled by a Persian subgovernor. Times had been difficult in Judah. To reconstruct the agricultural base for their economy, the people had scattered from Jerusalem and built smaller communities throughout the land. Even the Levites, dedicated to Temple service, had built homes and cleared land away from the city that was the site of their ministry. The walls of Jerusalem had not been rebuilt, and the people had begun to intermarry with the pagans of the land. This last act was a serious breach of Old Testament Law, which insisted that God's people maintain a separate identity. This was a very practical law; history demonstrates again and again that when the Israelites intermarried with pagans, the sure outcome was the introduction of idolatry.

Ezra wanted God's people to be freed from these harmful patterns of life and to be called back to the way God had laid out for them. No political reformer, Ezra was a teacher, "for Ezra had set his heart to study the law of the Lord, and to practice it, and to teach His statutes and ordinances in Israel" (Ezra 7:10). There was no doubt in Ezra's mind that a fresh start for God's people must be based on a return to His Word.

EZRA 7-10: HIGHLIGHTS	
Artaxerxes' decree	7:11-28
Ezra's prayer	9:5-15
The people's response	10:1-15

When Ezra returned, he came with a number of significant concessions from the king. Funds were granted so that sacrifices could be offered in Jerusalem for Artaxerxes and his sons. Those in Temple service were declared free from taxes. Ezra was given the right to appoint magistrates and other government officials, and the Old Testament Law was affirmed as the civil as well as religious code of the land. Praising God "who has put such a thing as this in the king's heart" (Ezra 7:27), Ezra and his company, after a time of fasting to ask God's protection on the long journey, set out for the homeland.

When the company finally arrived, Ezra discovered that intermarriage was commonplace—that in fact the leaders of Israel were the worst offenders! In a model prayer of confession (Ezra 9) this earnest and godly man so moved the people that they determined to take the painful course of separating from their foreign wives. With this "covenant to put away all the wives and their children . . . according to the law" (Ezra 10:3), the Israelites made another fresh start.

NEHEMIAH

It was only thirteen years after Ezra's return that Nehemiah came. Nehemiah was a high official at the Persian court who, out of concern for Jerusalem,

NEHEMIAH: HIGHLIGHTS	
Prayer of confession	1:4-11
Rebuilding the walls: opposition	4:1—6:15
Worship of the restored people	8:1—9:38
Covenant of the fresh start	10:28-39
Reforms . . . again	13:1-31

asked and was given permission to serve as governor of that minor district. He served in Jerusalem twelve years, returned to Persia, and then came to Judah a second time to govern there.

Unlike Ezra the priest, Nehemiah exercised political power. Yet his colorful and decisive leadership dealt with more than merely restoring respectability to Jerusalem. (In those days, an unwalled city was viewed as minor and unimportant—a "shame.") Nehemiah also committed himself to purifying the life-style of God's people and bringing them into conformity with the Law. It is striking to note that even Ezra's presence the past thirteen years had not protected the people of Israel from the tendency to drift. By Nehemiah's time, intermarriage was again a problem, and doing business on the Sabbath was an established way of life.

Nehemiah's day. I suppose for most who read the Bible, the ancient Jewish state seems to be a broad and extended kingdom.

Actually, Israel in her days of greatness never ranked in size with the empires and kingdoms of the Near East. In Nehemiah's day this always-small land had shrunk even more; the district of Yehud (Judah) included only some 800 square miles. It

PALESTINE IN NEHEMIAH'S DAY

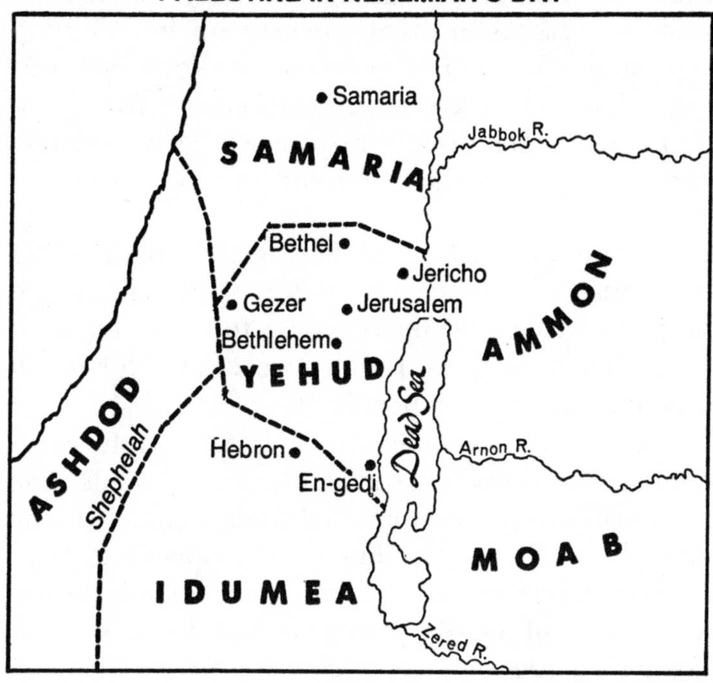

extended north and south about twenty-five miles and east and west about thirty-two. Nehemiah's choice of life on this insignificant parcel of land rather than in his important role in the Persian capital seems even more dramatic. And the plight of the exiles, surrounded on every side by hostile people, makes it easier for us to understand why Jewish morale often ebbed and why opposition from neighbors at times easily caused them to stop a project.

Nehemiah's boldness. But Nehemiah was of sterner stuff. On his return, he surveyed the tasks to be accomplished, laid his plans privately (2:11-16), and then boldly called the people of Israel to rebuild the walls of Jerusalem "that we may no longer be a reproach" (2:17). The response of the people was immediate—and so was the response of the opponents who were greatly displeased "that someone had come to seek the welfare of the sons of Israel" (2:10).

Bold seems to be the best word to describe Nehemiah's character. A catalog of the challenges he had to face, and his response to them, makes it clear that in spite of Judah's weakness Nehemiah was unimpressed by problems.

Nehemiah's commitment. Nehemiah brought great energy and courage to the building of the walls. The success of this project made a dramatic change in the attitude of the people. Their self-respect had been recovered by their victory over their enemies; their awareness of God's presence had been stirred. Gathering together to celebrate and praise God, Nehemiah put forward Ezra the scribe "to bring the book of the law of Moses, which the Lord had given to Israel" (8:1). All the people gathered to hear as Ezra read and interpreted the words. (Note: interpretation was necessary because by this time the language of the people was Aramaic, not the classical Hebrew of the Old Testament documents. Ezra and the other teachers had to read in the original, translate, and explain.)

The reading of the Law took some seven days and culminated on the eighth with a worship service. The Jews recovered a deep sense of their identity. They went on to express fresh commitment in a

Problem	Response
• ridicule by enemies	• asked God to vindicate them; ignored the ridicule
• plot to attack the builders	• set half the people to work, half to guard with arms in hand • encouraged Israel to remember the Lord
• poorer Jews borrowed from wealthy; they could not repay creditors while working on walls	• got wealthy to remit interest, return the lands taken as security • set example by supporting himself rather than demanding the governor's allowance
• invited to a "counsel" (trap) by the enemies	• refused to be distracted; kept building the walls
• Shemaiah the prophet hired by enemies to frighten Nehemiah into hiding in the Temple	• refused to hide from possible assassins; set example of courage
• threatened with a letter to Artaxerxes saying Nehemiah planned rebellion	• replied that the enemy had a good imagination; kept on with the work

written covenant (Neh. 10), which the leaders of the people signed. This covenant reflected those specific areas in which the people had drifted from God—and expressed their intention to observe the commandments of the Lord that they had previously ignored.

In a great outpouring of praise, Temple service

was restored, and the ministers of the Temple moved back to Jerusalem from their farms.

Nehemiah had not only led the people of Judah to rebuild the walls of their city; he had led them to renewed commitment to God and His revealed will.

Then comes Nehemiah 13.

Nehemiah had returned to Persia to report to the king. It is uncertain how long he was away, but when he returned, he was stunned by what he found. The fresh-start promises had been broken once again!

The people bought and sold on the Sabbath.

A guest room for one of Judah's pagan enemies had been prepared in the Temple of God itself!

Once again Jews had married foreign wives. "As for their children, half spoke in the language of Ashdod, and none of them was able to speak the language of Judah, but the language of his own people" (v. 24)!

Nehemiah's shock did not keep him from acting as boldly as ever. "I contended with them," Nehemiah reports, "and cursed them and struck some of them and pulled out their hair, and made them swear by God, 'You shall not give your daughters to their sons, nor take of their daughters for your sons or for yourselves' " (v. 25). And as for the grandson of the high priest, who was one of those who had married a foreign woman, "I drove him away from me" (v. 28).

Even the Levites had had to return to their land, because the people no longer paid the Temple tithes.

And here the Book of Nehemiah ends. "Thus I

purified them from everything foreign and appointed duties for the priests and the Levites. . . . Remember me, O my God, for good" (vv. 30-31).

And with these last words of Nehemiah, there comes a haunting question.

WHAT HAPPENED TO SPRINGTIME?

When God's people returned, they were full of hope, looking ahead, straining toward their destiny. Now that sense of destiny seems to have been lost. Even in the prayers of Ezra and Nehemiah, the focus seems to be on the past and present, not on the future. The reforms instituted in a surge of commitment are all too soon forgotten. The same dreary patterns of sin recur. Is it possible that the emphasis we see in these books of reform is essential—but not enough?

Is it possible that for you and me, too, a commitment to live our daily lives in God's way, while essential, is also not enough? Perhaps we too need more than a concentration on each succeeding "today" to keep our own hearts on God's upward path.

Today is important.

But somehow we need to maintain as well a growing sense of destiny. A sense of straining forward toward a goal: a goal that gives a meaning to life, that is not summed up in an endless repetition of days and nights like those we have known and our fathers have known before us. A goal that calls us to a fresh kind of preparation each new day for the destiny that *is* coming to meet us.

GOING DEEPER

to personalize

1. There are many meaningful lessons for us in Ezra and Nehemiah. Before going on, stop to read the *highlights* of each book, listed in the charts on pages 39 and 40. Underline what seems significant.

2. Do you ever feel the need for a fresh start? Think a bit about the following:

- When am I most likely to feel the need for a fresh start?
- What fresh starts would I like to make now?
- What is hard for me about making fresh starts?

3. How would you react to this statement? *There is no use making fresh starts, because I'm just going to fall back into old patterns of life anyway.* Either write briefly in *agreement* with the above, using Judah as an example. Or write briefly in *disagreement* with the above, using Nehemiah as an example.

4. Looking at relevant passages in both Ezra 7-10 and Nehemiah, how would you describe the role of each of the following in making a fresh start in recommitment to God? (1) Scripture, (2) confession, and (3) commitment.

to probe

1. One factor is important when we think of groups (rather than individuals) making a fresh start: the leader. Ezra and Nehemiah were both leaders, and yet were very different men. Write a three-to-five-page paper about the leadership of these two. Compare them to each other, and also

contrast them. What personality traits did each exhibit? How do you visualize them—warm, cold, calm, passionate, etc? Particularly study how each *moved others to respond,* for this is, of course, the key task of all leaders.

2. The fresh start as we have seen it in these two books seems to involve discovering God's will in the Word, confessing the faults and sins we need to reject, and expressing our commitment to His will—often done in the Old Testament in the form of a covenant promise.

For your own benefit (not to hand in), if you are aware of any areas in which you need to make a fresh start, why not *write out* your own confession and your own covenant, and present them to God now? Judah as a people turned away from their covenant; Nehemiah never did. You and I do not have to recapitulate the experience of Judah. We *can* be Nehemiahs!

4

Malachi

JOURNEY DOWNWARD

MALACHI, THE LAST BOOK of the Old Testament, is a discouraging document. The days of Ezra and Nehemiah are past, and no imprint seems to be left on the people of Judah. Again we find them sliding down toward sin and spiritual lethargy, trapped in the old patterns, but now completely indifferent to Malachi's call to another fresh start.

Haggai ended his book with words of hope: the kingdoms of this earth are about to be shaken, and God's servants will be worn by Him as a signet ring, "for I have chosen you, declares the Lord of hosts" (Hag. 2:23). Malachi ends on a note of warning and near despair. God must send another Elijah to His people before that great and terrible day of the Lord; the people must be reconciled not only to Him but to one another, "lest I come and smite the land with a curse" (Mal. 4:6). Reading this book, the last testimony to the men and women of the return, a peculiar realization grows. God's people have lost their vision of springtime. And when that vision is lost, a surrender to winter's grip is sure.

This is important for us to grasp, because the principle applies to you and me as well as to Israel. We too are forced to live with imperfection—our own imperfection as well as that of those around us! It is so easy to become discouraged when we try, and try again, and still seem to fail.

I remember the frustration my children felt when they were younger. Paul wanted to push our old man-powered lawnmower when he was five. And he couldn't. When he was twelve, he wanted desperately to beat me at basketball. And he couldn't do it (then). Tim sometimes feels deep frustration because he can't draw as well as his older brother, who is an artist. He tries, but his hands just can't form the lines as he sees them in his mind's eye. From the first stumbling steps of the toddler, and his tears when he falls, on through the teenage athlete's crushing defeat, life teaches us that we haven't arrived yet.

And yet with each child I've known that destiny lay ahead. "Soon you'll grow stronger." "Soon you'll grow tall." "Soon. . . ."

And it never seemed like soon.

And yet each child knew it was true.

I think there is an important analogy here for us in our spiritual experience. We are not yet what we shall be. And what we shall be always lies just beyond our grasp . . . our destiny is always ahead. But what is ahead *is* our destiny, and we can stretch out now, straining toward it. What's more, we're not doomed to remain as we are until destiny comes. We can grow toward it: *God calls us to grow toward it.* Like the toddler who stumbles, we are called to get up, to put our hand in our Father's, and to try again. In spite of our stumbling steps, each one we take does bring us closer to what we will be.

When we lose sight of destiny, and when we fail to grasp the reality of growth, our motivation to live for God begins to die. This is what happened to the people of Judah in Malachi's day. They had looked inward, lost sight of the destiny ahead, and abandoned hope for personal growth and change.

MALACHI'S DAY

Little is known about the prophet himself. But his writings give us a sharp portrait of conditions in Judah. The hard years seem to have passed. The city and its walls have been raised, the Temple rebuilt. Prosperity as well as relative independence from the peoples around them has returned. God's people have settled down into a good life in the land of Palestine.

But with blessing has come a peculiar reaction. The sense of need for God has receded; the yearning for the coming destiny has disappeared. God Himself is ignored, and even despised. All the meaning of life seems summed up in the experience of the good things of this world's *now.*

Malachi's book is organized around a series of seven sarcastic questions posed by the people of God in response to His words to them. These questions show a definite rejection of the divine viewpoint;

they show how far Judah's loss of a sense of destiny has caused them to drift.

In looking at these questions, it is easy to see some of our own attitudes reflected. In God's response we can hear His call, inviting us to turn our steps again toward our destiny.

Love lost (Mal. 1:1-5). The book begins with an affirmation: "I have loved you," says the Lord (v. 2). What a starting point for our relationship with God! It is not that we loved God; He loved us and, acting in love, delivered His people.

Yet the people of Malachi's day replied with a plaintive whine: "How hast Thou loved us?" (v. 2). It is as though a child, used to plenty, complains because he's been denied some new toy. With all the evidence of history and with all their present prosperity, Judah could still ask for proof of God's love!

God's answer is to point to the fact that He *chose* their ancestor Jacob over his twin Esau (who was the ancestor of the surrounding peoples). God's love was demonstrated primarily in that He chose to establish a relationship with this people; love draws us to Himself.

The phrase "I have hated Esau" (v. 3) bothers many here. It seems best to understand this expression not as a statement of feeling or attitude but as a *legal* term. In that day a father used this terminology in legally designating one son to inherit his possessions, while decisively rejecting the claim of another. By custom such a rejected son was cared for and given resources to make his own way. But the loved son inherited.

Honor denied (Mal. 1:6-9). God's complaint with Judah is that although He has called them into a relationship with Himself, the people have refused to honor Him. This goes beyond disrespect; they have "despised" God's name (v. 6). A son honors his father—and God has been a Father to Judah. A servant shows respect to his master; and God is called "Lord" and "Master" by His people. Why then is He treated as unimportant?

The people of Judah rejected this charge with another sarcasm. You can almost hear the tone of outraged innocence: "How have we despised Thy name?" (v. 6).

And God points to the mildewed bread on His Temple altar, to the ill and injured animals offered as sacrifice. They were offering to God what they wouldn't dare present to a human governor!

Worship defiled (Mal. 1:10-14). Worship involves essentially an expression of our realization of who God is; it is honoring and praising Him for Himself. Any true worship must honor and exalt Him.

Now we see the priests and Levites, who were to be closest to God and serve Him (and in return be cared for from the sacrifices and offerings brought to the Temple), complaining about their lot. They were unsatisfied with the offerings that God had chosen for Himself; they wanted the kind of food others ate. They were bored with worship (v. 13), and the people constantly sought to swindle God out of what they had vowed to Him.

Obedience ignored (Mal. 2:1-12). In this passage God reminds Judah that in the Sinai Covenant He promised the obedient that He would bless them. The Law outlined His plan for holy living, but they have not taken His ways to heart (v. 2). If they had only chosen to live by the Law, they would know life and peace and righteousness (v. 5). But the very priests charged with teaching God's way deny it—first with their actions (v. 8) and then in their distorted teaching of God's truth (v. 9).

This corruption cannot be overlooked. In spite of their relationship as the people of God, they are faithless and cruel to one another and faithless to the God they claim as their common Father.

Prayer unanswered (Mal. 2:13-16). When God warns Judah that He will not answer their prayers, their response is a complaining "Why does he not?" (v. 14, RSV). Here another sin of the people, another indication of their hardheartedness toward each other is brought into focus. They have initiated divorce as a societal life-style—not a divorce stimulated by one person's sin, but one motivated by an older man's desire for a new and young wife! This kind of faithlessness is something God cannot stand.

Evil affirmed (Mal. 2:17–3:4). Malachi's charge that Judah has "wearied the Lord with your words" stimulates another mock query: "How have we wearied Him?" Malachi's answer goes to the roots of another symptom of sickness in society. "In that you say, 'Everyone who does evil is good in the sight of the Lord' " (2:17).

How quickly humanistic values replace God's revelation of true goodness and purity. In our modern doubletalk, pornographic movies are called "mature," and great campaigns are launched to present homosexuality as an alternate and perfectly acceptable life-style. In Malachi's day too, society slipped into the practice of calling evil good.

This last charge leads Malachi to a promise and a warning. " 'He is coming,' says the Lord of hosts. 'But who can endure the day of His coming? And who can stand when He appears' " (3: 1, 2). Destiny, in the person of God's great Messenger, is approaching, and He will purify the land by judgment. *Then* the offerings of the remnant will be pleasing to God.

When we refuse to purify ourselves, God must do it in spite of us. It is not pleasant to be placed over what Malachi calls the "refiner's fire" (3: 2).

Return rejected (Mal. 3: 6-12). Approaching the end of the dialogue, God now confronts Judah with a call to restoration. "Return to me, and I will return to you, says the Lord of hosts." But the hardened people respond, "How shall we return?" (v. 7). The meaning of the question is clear: "What do you mean, *return!* Why, we've never strayed!"

So again God brings into focus evidence of their desertion of His path. They have been robbing Him of the tithes and offerings commanded in the Law. They can return by once again putting God first, and . . . if they will . . . God will open the very windows of heaven and pour out blessings. Not because they "paid" for them, but because, when God's people are close to Him, He enjoys doing them good.

The Lord denied (Mal. 3:13-15). One final word remains: God calls Judah to account for attacking

Him personally. And again the whining reply: "What have we spoken against Thee?" The answer: "You have said, 'It is vain to serve God' " (vv. 13-14).

They have *chosen* to set God aside as irrelevant; they have determined to pay Him no more attention. They may go through the motions. After all, appearance at the Temple is one of those things a well-bred person does. But in their hearts there is no longer a place for God.

Malachi ends with two special notes. First, he reports that while the society refused to turn to God, there were individuals "who gave attention and heard." And Malachi tells us that their names were recorded in God's record book (3:16-18). " 'They will be Mine,' says the Lord of hosts, 'on the day that I prepare My own possession.' "

And Malachi then shares a promise. "The day is coming, burning like a furnace; and all the arrogant and every evildoer will be chaff" (4:1). Destiny is approaching for the good and for the evil alike. Destiny is rushing toward us; we may fail to welcome it, but we shall not escape.

DESTINY

When we see it as springtime and reach out toward it with yearning, destiny helps direct and purify our lives. If we ignore it, if we focus our lives on this world and its pleasures and let our hearts be drawn away from God, then destiny is still ahead. But destiny then turns into searing heat.

Invitation. Stimulation to a fresh kind of life now.

Or warning. Exhortation to change before it is too late.

Each of these elements can be found in the Bible's portrait of the destiny that lies ahead for mankind . . . and for each individual.

So far in this **Bible Alive Series** we have not explored prophecy's picture of the future. We're about to do that now. Looking at the history of the people who returned from the Exile full of hope that they would find fulfillment in their ancient land, we can see compellingly why we must. Just as history gives us our sense of identity, an awareness of who we are in relationship to God, so prophecy gives us our sense of destiny, an awareness of who we will become.

Maintaining a sense of destiny seems to me the only way to keep life in balance. I must know where I am going to be able to place each step along the way. I must have hope for tomorrow to free me to accept God's fresh-start invitations when I stumble today. And I must, in the face of wars and all the tragic evidence of society's breakdown, have a firm conviction that history is moving down its God-intended path. In the promise of God's full restoration of justice and joy I can find strength.

Destiny ahead.

In these next chapters, we'll see its shape.

GOING DEEPER

to personalize

1. Malachi is an excellent book to help us examine

MALACHI STUDY CHART		
Issue	Judah's pattern	Modern patterns

ourselves and our patterns of response to God. Use the above chart: read each passage, fill in Judah's pattern, and then in the third column spell out modern patterns (that is, ways this same kind of problem finds expression in our society today).

2. Study carefully Malachi 3:16—4:5. How does God seem to use these pictures of destiny coming? From just this passage alone, how many possible values can you think of for having a clear impression of what the Bible teaches about the future?

3. Without looking beyond this passage, jot down your present ideas about what is ahead. Particularly, what do you think God's plan for the end of the world might involve—if there is such a plan? Later you'll be able to compare your sketch with the portrait we'll develop from the Old Testament prophets.

to probe

1. In God's response to the people of Malachi's day, He brought out evidence—of His love, or of their failure to respond. Pick three of the seven areas on the chart (above), and write briefly on New Testament parallels. That is, what kind of evidence might God point to of His love or of our response to Him from the perspective of His New Testament revelation in Christ?

2. In a later book *(The Servant King,* the first of the New Testament books of this series), the intertestamental period is briefly sketched. This includes those centuries between the writing of Malachi, about 400 B.C., and the period reported in the Gospels. Find a book or check a resource such as the *Zondervan Pictorial Encyclopedia of the Bible* and read about this period between the Testaments. It will help you trace the history of the Jews through a period many people are ignorant of.

Part Two

HISTORY AHEAD

5

Daniel 1–7

VISIONS IN THE NIGHT

THE BIBLE IS A BOOK of history. Archaeological discovery after discovery has shown just how accurate it is; we can trust Scripture's historical accounts.

But the Bible is more. Among its amazing claims is the clear expression of confidence that its writers and prophets are inspired by God to predict the future. Sometimes these predictions are narrow and specific, touching the life of an individual or the near future of a city or nation. But often prediction involves vast and sweeping panoramas, encompassing the destiny of not only the nations of our world but of the universe itself. In these next chapters we'll look at the shape of history ahead as the Bible describes it, and in the last section of our study focus on the "end times"—the culmination of history as it is portrayed in the Old Testament.

How confident can we be that the Bible's picture of history ahead is accurate? Probably the best way is to look closely at the life and writings of one man: Daniel.

DANIEL

As a young teenager, Daniel and several friends were taken to Babylon in the first group of captives (597 B.C.). There Daniel was trained with young men from other districts of the far-flung empire for the Babylonian civil service. Through a series of events recorded in his book, Daniel was advanced to the highest positions in the administration of three empires, and his lifetime spans the entire period of Judah's captivity.

Five incidents illustrate Daniel's relationship with these world rulers: his decision not to defile himself with pagan foods (chap. 1, 597 B.C.), his interpretation of Nebuchadnezzar's first dream (chap. 2, 595 B.C.) his interpretation of Nebuchadnezzar's second dream (chap. 4, ca. 567 B.C.), his reading of the writing on Belshazzar's wall, when Daniel was at least eighty (chap. 5, 539 B.C.), and his being cast into the lions' den (chap. 6, ca. 537 or 536 B.C.).

In addition, Daniel experienced at least four times of revelation of future history. Those recorded in chapters 7—9 probably were given during Belshazzar's reign, while those in chapters 10—12 were in the first and third years of Cyrus' reign.

Of particular note is the fact that the Book of Daniel is written half in Hebrew and half in Aramaic, the language of the Gentile world of Daniel's day. The Aramaic portion, chapters 2:4—7:28, which we'll focus on in this chapter, seems addressed to the Gentile world.

Daniel the man. Daniel is portrayed as a distinctly

committed and humble man. Although he rose to the highest governmental rank and was familiar with several world rulers, Daniel maintained his daily walk with God. His character is mentioned several times by Ezekiel, a contemporary of his, who compares his righteousness to Noah's and Job's (Ezek. 14:14, 20). Daniel is set up by Ezekiel as the standard against which to measure wisdom (Ezek. 28:3). When jealous enemies tried to set Daniel aside from his administrative posts, they could find no areas of weakness except that he was faithful to God. Their attempt to turn Daniel's commitment to their own advantage—and how that attempt backfired!—is recorded in the famous story of Daniel and the lions' den.

Daniel's times. Probably the Book of Daniel has been given more critical scrutiny than any of the prophetic books of the Old Testament. Some scholars have believed that it was not written by Daniel at all, but by an unknown author about 165 B.C. The main reason for this belief is the amazing detail with which Daniel outlines history, at least to the times of Antiochus in the 160s. Those who cannot accept the idea of supernatural revelation of the future have been forced to seek some other explanation for Daniel's accuracy!

Yet the book itself claims to be Daniel's work, and Jesus authenticates his prophecies (see Matt. 24:15; Mark 13:14). Fragments of Daniel's book have been found in the Qumran documents—a cache of Old Testament books dating from the early first and second centuries A.D.—and it is highly unlikely that "fiction" would have been included among that community's treasure-house of Scripture.

Actually, as Leon Wood points out, many recent archaeological discoveries strongly support the Daniel authorship and the exilic dating. Wood summarizes,

> The author shows remarkable knowledge of Babylonian and early Persian history, such as would be true of a contemporary like Daniel. In the fourth chapter Nebuchadnezzar is presented correctly as the creator of the Neo-Babylonian empire. In the fifth chapter Belshazzar is set forth as co-ruler of Babylon, a fact only recently demonstrated by archaeological research. In the sixth chapter, Darius is presented as ruler of Babylon, even though Cyrus was the supreme ruler of Persia; Cyrus is now known to have appointed one Gubaru in this capacity, with whom Darius may well be identified. In the second chapter (cf. vv. 12, 13, 46) Nebuchadnezzar is shown to have been able to change Babylonian laws which he had previously made (such a change is now known to have been possible in Babylonia); whereas in the sixth chapter (cf. vv. 8, 9, 12, 15) Darius is presented as not having been able to do this (such a change is now known to have been impossible in Persia).[1]

The supernatural. The only serious question left concerning the authenticity of Daniel has to do with the likelihood of the supernatural. The book describes several notable miracles. God delivers Shadrach, Meshach, and Abed-nego (three Jewish fellow-captives) from a fiery furnace. Through Daniel, God not only interprets Nebuchadnezzar's dream; He even describes the dream when Nebuchadnezzar has refused to reveal it to his "wise men" advisers. The mouths of a den of hungry lions are closed by angelic intervention to preserve Daniel's life . . . and then opened to crush the bones of Daniel's enemies. Nebuchadnezzar is struck with seven years' madness, and when he recovers his throne is returned.

How likely are these amazing events? How much confidence can we place in miracle?

This is, of course, the same argument raised against prophecy. No living human being can possibly know the outline of the future, and certainly not in the detail given in a Bible book like Daniel. If we reject the idea that God exists or that He acts in the world of men, then of course we have to seek some other explanation for miracle. We have to suppose that people who describe historical events live *after* they have happened rather than before.

But once we admit the possibility of the supernatural. . . ! Once we accept the fact that God may actually *not* be standing impotently on the outside of space and time . . . then everything changes. *If God exists, and if He is the kind of God the Bible describes, then there is nothing impossible about miracles and nothing unlikely about prophecy.*

In fact, the Bible records four great but relatively short outbursts of miracles. The first is the time of miracles associated with the deliverance of Israel from Egyptian bondage (the Exodus). The second is in the days of Elijah and Elisha, just after the unified kingdom of Israel had been broken in two. The third is focused on the times of Daniel. The fourth is the days of Jesus and the early church. Through most of recorded time God did not choose to intervene in obvious ways; He chose instead the quiet providential guiding of events as illustrated by the experience of Esther.

Why then the periods of miracle? Some have suggested that miracles seem to be associated with times of deep-set resistance to God with questioning of God's power. In Daniel's time the miracles certainly had these two functions of witness and reassurance. To the Babylonians, a god was evaluated by the size of the nation worshiping him and the power of that nation's army. How could the God of insignificant Judah, whose people had been led away in humiliation, be anything but insignificant too?

And then, as Daniel records the series of miraculous interventions, we see a gradual change in the attitude of the Babylonian rulers! Finally even Nebuchadnezzar himself is seen praising and honoring the Most High,

> "For His dominion is an everlasting dominion,
> And His kingdom endures from generation to generation.
> And all the inhabitants of the earth are accounted as nothing,
> But He does according to His will in the host of heaven
> And among the inhabitants of the earth;
> And no one can ward off His hand
> Or say to Him, 'What hast Thou done?' "
>
> *Daniel 4:34, 35*

We can see how such rulers' public decrees acknowledging God must have comforted the captives. Had their God lost power, or lost His love for them? No, even in captivity they were not abandoned! Even here God acted and in His miracles gave continuing testimony to His involvement in their lives.

You or I may choose to hold a view of God that denies Him the power to intervene in space and time, or that at least doubts His will to do so. But it is clear that the writers of the Bible held no such limited view. The God of the Bible chose to stand behind the scenes of history for the most part. But when He chooses, He can and will intervene. And even behind the scenes, He is the Author and Director of the play. So history moves, purposefully, toward the great climax He has planned.

IMPACT ON HIS OWN TIME

Like all Old Testament prophets, Daniel had a great impact on his own era. Unlike most, Daniel's impact was primarily on the very highest ranks of *pagan* rulers.

Earlier, the experience of Jonah had shown that God cares for pagan peoples as well as for His chosen community of Israel (see especially Jonah 4). In Daniel we see God acting in grace in the lives of pagan individuals to bring them to a knowledge of Himself. The apparent conversion of Nebuchadnezzar is among the most striking of all Old Testament events, particularly when contrasted to

Pharaoh's response some thousand years earlier.

At the same time, Daniel must have had several very vital influences on the captive Israelites. His early example of commitment to God (Dan. 1) was an encouraging testimony to the fact that the believer could remain true to his faith in a pagan culture—and still find acceptance and even advancement. Rather than withdrawing from his world, Daniel influenced the course of events.

Often questions are raised today about the validity of Christians in politics. Shouldn't the true believer withdraw from the system, particularly when to get ahead seems associated with compromise and questionable "yokes" with unbelievers? While this is not a simple question, the experience of Daniel demonstrates that when God calls a believer to a role within the power structure of society, that individual can both remain true to God *and* influence the course of history.

It is possible, as some have suggested, that the influence of Daniel even extended to drafting Cyrus's decree permitting the first groups of Jews to return to Jerusalem to rebuild the Temple. If so, this must have been one of the final—and most satisfying—acts of Daniel's long and useful life.

Daniel's righteousness, described by Ezekiel as being legendary in his own day, stood to the exiles as a beacon, pointing them toward the way to live for God no matter where they might be.

One final influence on His own people must have come from the prophetic sections of the book he authored (chaps. 7—12). Daniel was old when these sections were introduced. The Jews had been in Babylon for a generation or more. After the passage of decades, the majority would have settled down to seek the best possible adjustment to their fate. Many would have been born and grown to maturity there knowing nothing of their homeland or their God except what was passed on by tradition. For a great many of that generation, Hebrew was a foreign tongue; even by the time of Ezra and Nehemiah it was necessary for the scholar to explain in Aramaic what the original text meant.

But God's people were not meant to settle down in a foreign land. Destiny awaited them, and the whole world, in Palestine!

Someday Messiah would come. Someday the kingdoms of this world would be shaken. Someday all worldly glory would be shattered. There would come one "like a Son of Man" (Dan. 7:13). To Him, the Ancient of Days would make a great presentation; looking ahead in a great vision of the night Daniel saw destiny.

> And to Him was given dominion,
> Glory and a kingdom,
> That all the peoples, nations, and men of every
>   language
> Might serve Him.
> His dominion is an everlasting dominion
> Which will not pass away;
> And His kingdom is one
> Which will not be destroyed.
>
> *Daniel 7:14*

Through Daniel, the vision of the earlier prophets was confirmed to captive Israel, and the Jews were invited once again to strain forward toward the coming destiny.

GOING DEEPER

to personalize

1. Read quickly the first seven chapters of Daniel and enjoy the graphic descriptions of the unique events and relationships that marked this man's life.

2. Go back now and restudy chapters 2—4, which tell of Daniel's relationship with Nebuchadnezzar. From these chapters see if you can (a) develop a sketch of Daniel's own commitments, and (b) see principles that might guide others to influence persons who are of higher rank or status.

3. What's your opinion? Should a believer become involved in politics? Why, or why not? (Are Daniel's rather special circumstances analogous to modern political involvements?)

4. In chapter 7 Daniel reports a striking dream he had during the reign of Belshazzar. *Without looking in any commentary or guide,* how might you understand or interpret what is written here? Soon we'll look at principles for the interpretation of Bible prophecy. But for now, try to think through this passage on your own. For instance, it might help if you jotted down lists of what you *do* understand and what you *do not* understand. Also, be careful at the beginning to specify the *subject* apparently in view.

to probe

1. Check several Old Testament introduction books to see why some believe and some reject Daniel's authorship.

2. Review the time period and get firmly in mind the relationship of Daniel to his contemporaries. How, for instance, are Daniel, Jeremiah, and Ezekiel related to the history of this period? What is the contribution and thrust of each?

1. Leon Wood, *A Commentary on Daniel* (Grand Rapids: Zondervan, 1972), p. 20.

6

Daniel 7–8

"I DECLARE NEW THINGS"

THE BIBLE NEVER SHIES AWAY from the supernatural. Its writers never claimed to be struggling toward an understanding of God. Instead they claimed to be ordinary men to whom the God behind the universe had made a unique revelation of Himself.

The apostle Paul, quoting the Old Testament, summed up this supernatural presupposition this way:

> "No eye has seen,
> no ear has heard,
> no mind has conceived
> what God has prepared for those who love him—"
> but God has revealed it to us by his Spirit.
>
> *1 Corinthians 2:9, 10*

This notion that God has revealed information not available to man through natural sources is the consistent position of the Scriptures. One evidence is found in Bible prophecy.

In fact, Isaiah contrasts the Lord with the idols and false gods the Jewish people had turned to on this specific point: they are dumb . . . He foretells the future.

> Let them bring forth and declare to us what is going to take place;
> As for the former events, declare what they were,
> That we may consider them, and know their outcome;
> Or announce to us what is coming.
> Declare the things that are going to come afterward,
> That we may know that you are gods;
> Indeed, do good or evil, that we may anxiously look about us and fear together.
> Behold, you are of no account,
> And your work amounts to nothing;
>
> . . .
>
> "I am the Lord; that is My name;
> I will not give my glory to another,
> Nor My praise to graven images.
> Behold, the former things have come to pass,
> Now I declare new things;
> Before they spring forth I proclaim them to you."
>
> *Isaiah 41:22-23; 42:8-9*

God alone, through His servants the prophets,

preannounced "the former things," and they *did* come to pass just as foretold. It is this God of the Scriptures who declares the "new things" before they spring into being.

THE PURPOSE OF PROPHECY

It is clear from Isaiah's impassioned plea to the people of his own day that one function of prophecy is to encourage God's people to trust Him. Predictions that *always come to pass* are clear indications that there is something beyond nature. They are also evidence that the Supernatural either knows the future—or controls the future!

But prophecy in the Scriptures is more than evidence for belief in God. Prophecy says something about God's involvement in lives of His people.

Deuteronomy 18: 9-22. This passage contains one of the most significant instructions given by Moses just before Israel passed over the Jordan River into the Promised Land. God's people had just been delivered from Egyptian slavery; they were about to enter a settled land with a culture marked by a profusion of gods and goddesses. These were mainly nature gods, associated with the cycle of the season and the fertility of the land and people. Some of the practices associated with this faith, called by God "abominable practices," are seen in the divine prohibitions that focus on practices of the occult.

> You shall not learn to follow the abominable practices of those nations. There shall not be found

among you any one who burns his son or his daughter as an offering, any one who practices divination, a soothsayer, or an augur, or a sorcerer, or an charmer, or a medium, or a wizard, or a necromancer. For whoever does these things is an abomination to the Lord.

Deuteronomy 18:9-12 (RSV)

There was then, and still is, a deep human attraction to the occult. Each of us at times senses the frustrations of the limits of our nature; each of us wants some insight, some guidance, some kind of supernatural assurance that our choices are good ones, or that at least everything will come out all right in the end. Tarot cards and Ouija boards may be different means than were used by the ancients, but the purpose is the same. Astrology has hardly changed at all. Through these means people reach out to grasp something beyond the natural, something supernatural to bring them aid.

In this Deuteronomy passage God strictly forbids an appeal to the occult by His people. Yes, there *is* a supernatural world, and through the occult it may be contacted. But the contact is with evil, not good!

What is more, the believer is *not* cut off from contact with the supernatural. In fact, contact is invited . . . with God. God seeks a *personal relationship* with man—not a relationship initiated by us through questionable intermediaries, but a direct relationship initiated by God. The breakthrough into the supernatural is made by Him from His side of the barrier, not by us from our side. So Deuteronomy promises just the kind of guidance and help we would long for. Moses goes on:

> The Lord your God will raise up for you a prophet like me from among you, from your countrymen, you shall listen to Him. . . . And I [the Lord] will put My words in his mouth, and he shall speak to them all that I command him.
>
> *Deuteronomy 18:15, 18*

The prophetic movement in Israel was not primarily to authenticate the supernatural. Rather it developed in fulfillment of God's promise to speak to His people whenever they needed fresh guidance. God committed Himself to speak to the Old Testament believers through the prophets.

The prophets' ministry. Tracing through the Old Testament, we can see several characteristics of the prophets' ministry. First, it was primarily religious. The prophets did not normally speak about when to plant crops or when to harvest. They occasionally guided military activities, but their main focus was on the ongoing relationship of the people with their Lord. Again and again we hear the prophets rebuke concerning sin and promise restoration when there is a turning to God's ways.

Second, we note that the prophets' words always spring from the context of their own times and are addressed to their own contemporaries. In our last survey study (*Edge of Judgment*), we looked at the ministry of a number of prophets and saw the impact of their messages on their own society.

Third, as we will see increasingly in this study, Old Testament prophecy is definitely predictive. It is teleological: it looks forward toward an end, a culmination. What is said to a contemporary generation is said *in view of a destiny* the prophet sees as fast approaching.

Old Testament prophecy was not an everyday kind of thing. In those days as in ours, the believer was to walk by faith in obedience to the written Word. Yet whenever history seemed to take a turn away from God, or when special help and guidance was necessary, God's promised messenger did appear.

The messengers. The Bible speaks of both false and true prophets and tells how to distinguish between them. (1) The true prophet was "from your countrymen" (Deut. 18:18): a Hebrew. (2) The true prophet spoke in the name of Jehovah—not in the name of Baal or another god. (3) The true prophet's commission would be validated by prediction.

> "And you may say in your heart, 'How shall we know the word which the Lord has not spoken?' When a prophet speaks in the name of the Lord, if the thing does not come about or come true, that is the thing which the Lord has not spoken. The prophet has spoken it presumptuously; you shall not be afraid of him."
>
> *Deuteronomy 18:21-22*

Here is a decisive test. What he speaks must *always* come true! If his predictions do not come to pass, then his words can be discounted, and he need not be heeded.

This helps to account for an interesting phenomonon. Even those prophets who deal with the most far-flung future, focusing nearly all their attention on the end of time, also speak short-term prophecies. It is these prophecies, whose accuracy can be attested by the prophet's contemporaries, that establish him as God's spokesman.

No wonder the Book of Daniel records not only the miraculous interpretation of Nebuchadnezzar's first dream but also the prophecy of Nebuchadnezzar's coming madness. Within a year, what Daniel foretold did come to pass; within seven more the king was restored to his throne, and then he recognized God as Lord. With credentials established by prophecies that could be tested within the prophet's own time, Daniel's portrait of the future would be studied with wonder . . . and with belief.

It is even more striking for us, looking back over the centuries, to see the accuracy with which Daniel outlined centuries of world history between his own day and the coming of Jesus. Surely God can boldly proclaim:

> "Behold, the former things have come to pass,
> Now I declare new things;
> Before they spring forth, I proclaim them to you."
> *Isaiah 42:9*

DANIEL: HISTORY AHEAD

Daniel 7–8

These two chapters, one of which you read last week, contain prophecies that came as visions to Daniel and were interpreted for him. Each has to do with the same events; the doubling of the prophecy speaks of its certainty.

It is clear that the focus is on governments: four world empires. The first is that of Nebuchadnezzar; the second is Cyrus's Media-Persian empire; and the third is the Greek (Hellenistic) empire won by Alexander the Great and, on his death, divided among four of his generals. The fourth empire is not identified, but in the sequence of history it is clear that this must be the Roman.

It is also clear that visions of Daniel 7 and 8 correspond with the vision of the great statue recorded in Daniel 2.

Each of these three prophetic teachings focuses on the Gentile world powers that are to rule as history marches toward its culmination. In each teaching, the fourth empire is to be replaced by a kingdom set up by the Lord of Heaven.

- In Daniel 2, we have the picture of a stone cut without tools from a mountain, which dashes the previous governments into pieces and grows to fill the whole earth.
- In Daniel 7, we have the picture of the Ancient of Days seated in judgment, destroying the final enemy. Then, "with the clouds of heaven," a "Son of Man" comes to receive dominion and glory and kingdom. He rules forever.

• In Daniel 8, we again see the final enemy destroyed by the Prince of princes . . . but only after the very sanctuary of God has suffered revolting sacrilege (v. 13).

This later prophecy is not explained to Daniel, for his angelic interpreter reports that "the vision pertains to the time of the end" (8:17).

It is in fact these prophecies, with their accurate portrayal of the history of the fifth through second centuries B.C., that have led many to question Daniel's authorship of the book. How could such details as the death of Alexander and the division of his kingdom be told *before* the fact? To anyone unwilling to admit the supernatural, there must be some alternate explanation. Especially in view of the *detailed* accuracy of the prophecy, commented on here in this extended quote by Leon Wood:

> 8:8 Thus the he-goat became very great; but when he was strong the great horn was broken, and in place of it came up four winds of heaven.
>
> *Became very great:* This is the same phrase as used regarding the ram in verse four, except for the addition of "very." It could be translated "did very great things," but the thought would still be that the goat became very great, so as to be able to do them. The addition of the adverb, "very," is apparently meant to indicate that the he-goat became greater than the ram.
>
> *Great horn was broken:* Daniel does not state what happened in the vision to cause the great horn to be broken, but this detail is not needed to see the intended symbolism. Alexander dies when he had just subjected all Medo-Persia to himself. On returning to

FULFILLED PROPHECIES

Daniel 2, 7, 8

	Babylon (605-538 B.C.)	Medo-Persia (538-331 B.C.)	Greece (331-146 B.C.)	Rome (146 B.C.—A.D. 476)
Daniel 2:31-45 Dream image (603 B.C.)	Head of gold (2:32, 37, 38)	Breast, arms of silver (2:32, 39)	Belly, thighs of brass (2:32, 39)	Legs of iron Feet of iron and clay (2:33, 40, 41)
Daniel 7 First vision: Four Beasts (553 B.C.)	Lion (7:4)	Bear (7:5)	Leopard (7:6)	Strong Beast (7:7, 11, 19, 23)
Daniel 8 Second vision: Ram and goat (551 B.C.)		Ram (8:3, 4, 20)	Goat with one horn (8:5-8, 21) Four horns (8:8, 22) Little horn (8:9-14)	

Babylon from the east, he was taken with a severe fever, and in June, 323 B.C., died at the age of thirty-two. He had left his home country over eleven years before, and apparently never returned. He was taken in death, a young military genius, cut off at the height of achievement and power.

Four prominent horns: Where the great horn had been, Daniel now saw four take its place. The word for "prominent" is the same as that used in verse five, but it is used here without the preceding construct word "horn." Its use appears to be adverbial, giving the literal translation, "there came up prominently four in its place." This development is symbolic of the dividing of Alexander's vast holdings between four of his generals: Cassander receiving Macedonia and Greece; Lysimachus, Thrace and much of Asia Minor; Seleucus, Syria and vast regions to the east; and Ptolemy, Egypt. For a while a fifth, Antigonus, held territory in Asia Minor, but in 301 B.C. he was overthrown. It should be noted that the imagery employed in the vision does not imply, correctly, that Alexander himself divided the empire. He did not: the fourfold division came rather as a result of extensive fighting among the generals during twenty-two years.

The four winds: Reference is to the four directions: Cassander to the west, Lysimachus to the north, Seleucus to the east, and Ptolemy to the south.[1]

INTERPRETING PROPHECY

The extended quote from Leon Wood gives us several insights into the interpretation of prophecy.

First, we take very seriously each image and phrase . . . especially when the images are explained in the Bible text, as they are in 8:15-27.

Second, while the details are shown to be accurate, it is clear that in sketching the future *not all details are provided* (for instance, the way the great horn was broken, or the years of warfare before the four subsequent rulers were established in their "four winds" kingdoms).

Third, while there is sequence to the events, the time factor is not specified. In fact, uncertainty as to time is one of the most characteristic—and difficult—aspects of most Bible prophecy.

Can we develop some ground rules for reading and interpreting prophecy? The following are generally suggested:

General principles. As in understanding any passage of Scripture, there are a number of things to keep in mind:

1. The historical setting: out of what context is the author writing? For instance, it is appropriate that a man high in the government of the first great empire should be the channel through which the history of coming world powers would be outlined.

2. The words themselves are significant. At times prophecy, as here in Daniel, turns to figurative elements. The ram clearly *stood for* a world power. Often figurative elements are explained in text. At times they are not.

3. The context and flow of the passage is important. Our present verse and chapter divisions were not in the original manuscripts. These artificial breaks should not be blindly relied on.

4. The literary mold is important. Poetry has its own

logic and way of conveying meaning, a way that is different from descriptive prose. To say that we interpret the Bible "literally" does not mean treating poetry as if it were prose description.

5. Keep watch for parallels and cross-references. Important teachings are often repeated. Thus, finding correlated passages that add to or better define the larger picture is important. Such parallel passages will not contradict each other but will often help us avoid an oversimplification of the larger picture.

Specific problems. We have a number of specific difficulties in interpreting prophecy. Often the language seems somewhat ambiguous, and there is much too much prophetic literature to keep everything in focus. In addition, we are far outside the historical setting; meanings that may have been clear to the writers' contemporaries are less clear to us today.

What are some principles we can keep in mind to help us with our study of prophecy?

1. Determine if the passage is didactic or predictive. Is it describing something present or looking ahead? At times this is difficult to determine, as the prophet's viewpoint often shifts from the present into the future and back again.

2. Is the prophetic element conditional or unconditional? It is clear from Jonah's experience in Nineveh that prophecies are sometimes conditional. As God reminded Israel through Jeremiah:

> "At one moment I might speak concerning a nation or concerning a kingdom to uproot, to pull

down, or to destroy it, if that nation against which I have spoken, turns from its evil, I will relent concerning the calamity I planned to bring on it."

Jeremiah 18:7-8

Prophecy is often God's invitation to a wayward people to repent and avoid the disaster toward which it is headed.

Yet at other times there is the clear announcement that a prophetic warning is unconditional; that God will *not* divert the announced disaster.

3. Determine if the predictive prophecy is fulfilled or unfulfilled. This is also difficult at times, for Scripture sometimes follows the "law of double reference." That is, a warning or prediction may speak *both* of an event near at hand and a similar distant event. The Babylonian Captivity of Israel, in fulfillment of warnings given in Deuteronomy, was not the *only* scattering and dispersion Israel has known (as our own era attests).

4. Watch out for time gaps. I noted earlier that while the major events of the future seem to be sketched with clarity, the *time factor* is uncertain. This temporal uncertainty is a basic and critical aspect of Bible prophecy, well illustrated by Isaiah 61:1-2. There, speaking of the Messiah, the prophet cries out:

The Spirit of the Lord God is upon Me,
because the Lord has anointed me—
To bring good news to the afflicted;
He has sent me to bind up the brokenhearted,

To proclaim liberty to captives,
And freedom to prisoners;
To proclaim the favorable year of the Lord,
And the day of vengeance of our God.

In Luke 4 we hear Christ quoting these verses, identifying Himself as the promised Messiah. But after reading the word "to proclaim the year of the Lord's favor," the Bible tells us, "Then he rolled up the scroll" (Luke 4: 20)! He did not read ". . . and the day of vengeance of our God."

Why?

Because the day of vengeance had not yet come. 2 Thessalonians tells us the day is coming . . . when Christ returns (1: 7-9). What we have in Isaiah 61 is a prophecy about the Messiah's first *and second* coming . . . with no indication of the major time gap between "favor" and "and"!

Yet, with all the difficulties we face in struggling to understand Bible prophecy—with all the omitted details and all the uncertainty about time—one thing is clear. God has spoken about the future, *and those prophecies that have been fulfilled have been fulfilled literally.* As J. Dwight Pentecost has written, "In the field of fulfilled prophecy, it is not possible to point to any prophecy that has been fulfilled in any other way than literally."[2]

Often we must wait until history catches up with prophecy for a full understanding of all that God has planned. But when history does overtake the foretold future, we invariably discover how completely accurate prophecy has been.

CONCLUSIONS?

We might suggest several tentative conclusions at this point.

Since so much of the Scriptures is predictive (someone has suggested up to one sixth of the Bible is predictive), we cannot ignore the Bible's portrait of the future.

Since there are so many difficulties in interpreting prophecy, we must approach this task carefully—looking to already fulfilled prophecy to guide us.

Since uncertainty seems to grow both from (1) times and sequences and (2) incomplete descriptions of events, we must carefully avoid dogmatic schemes and systems. Yes, we *can* develop a picture of destiny from the Bible. In broad outline. But we should hesitate to fill in every detail, every event, every sequence of cause and effect. The details will become clear when destiny arrives. Until then we can know destiny is coming. We can know that God has a plan, that history has purpose and goal. And we can evaluate our own lives and our values in view of the destiny that most certainly approaches.

GOING DEEPER

to personalize

1. Read Daniel 2, 7, and 8 very carefully, working with the chart provided on page 81. What principles discussed on pages 83-86 can you see illustrated in your own study of these sections? Record your observations.

2. One particular challenge faces us in these

prophecies of Daniel. History seems to march toward an *end.* How does it happen that some two thousand years have passed and the Kingdom has not been established? Doesn't this indicate that Daniel is really just some later political document, and not prophecy at all? Do any of the principles on pages 83-86 help you with this problem? Do you see any clues in the text that might provide an answer?

3. Zechariah is a post-exilic prophet, a contemporary of Haggai. Zechariah's book covers the same prophetic period as Daniel, except that it is written from the point of view of the Jews rather than the Gentile powers. To sharpen your awareness of prophecy principles, study Zechariah 9: 9-17. What principles of prophecy do you see illustrated? How does this passage coordinate with what you read in Daniel 7 and 8?

to probe

1. Look up several books on prophecy, and see if they spell out their hermeneutics (principles of interpretation). List the principles that seem most important to you, and include illustrations.

2. Skim two or more commentaries on Daniel 7 and 8. What insights do they give that you did not get in your own reading of the text? Why do you think there were things you did not "see" in your own reading? (Note especially general principle number five on page 84 of this text.)

1. Leon Wood, *A Commentary on Daniel* (Grand Rapids: Zondervan, 1972), p. 211f.

2. J. Dwight Pentecost, *Things to Come* (Grand Rapids: Zondervan, 1958), p. 10.

7

Daniel 9–12

THE COMING PRINCE

JUST HOW ACCURATE is Bible prophecy? How sure can we be we've correctly understood a particular passage? The Book of Daniel gives unique evidence for Bible prophecy's amazing accuracy in one specific sequence that *does* specify the time factor. In fact, the timing is so clear that this prophecy gives us a great insight into God's overall plan as well as an explanation of why the promised destiny, the Messiah's kingdom, has not yet appeared.

In the years before the turn of the century, Sir Robert Anderson, a lay theologian and Bible teacher in Great Britain, could not agree with Germany's "higher critics," who attacked the accuracy and dating of many Old Testament documents. Anderson determined to study the subject, working from the language of Scripture itself and archaeological discoveries. (Thus, for instance, he used the 360-day sacred Jewish calendar rather than the Julian calendar in computing time.)

Working carefully, Anderson was able to pinpoint the exact day from which Daniel 9 says a specific period of time is to be counted.

> "Seventy weeks have been decreed for your people and your holy city, to finish the transgression, to make an end of sin, to make atonement for iniquity, to bring in everlasting righteousness, to seal up vision and prophecy, and to anoint the most holy place. So you are to know and discern that from the issuing of a decree to restore and rebuild Jerusalem until Messiah the Prince there will be seven weeks and sixty-two weeks; it will be built again, with plaza and moat, even in times of distress. Then after the sixty-two weeks the Messiah will be cut off and have nothing, and the people of the prince who is to come will destroy the city and the sanctuary. And its end will come with a flood; even to the end there will be war; desolations are determined. And he will make a firm covenant with the many for one week, but in the middle of the week he will put a stop to sacrifice and grain offering; and on the wing of abominations will come one who makes desolate, even until a complete destruction, one that is decreed, is poured out on the one who makes desolate."
>
> *Daniel 9:24-27*

ANDERSON'S CALCULATIONS

Sir Robert took each statement of Scripture and

sorted out the dates involved. The salient aspects of his interpretation are included on the chart on page 92, with the critical elements as follows:

Weeks. The word translated "weeks of years" (9:24, RSV) is *shabua,* meaning literally "sevens." The Jews used this term for weeks and also for a "sabbath of years," or seven years (see 2 Chron. 36:21; Gen. 29:27). Using the Hebrew religious year, Anderson determined that a period of 490 years was divided into two separate time periods:

69 weeks, or 173,880 days

1 week, or 2,520 days

When did this divine countdown begin? And when did the first period end?

The dating. Three decrees made possible the Jews' return to Palestine. The first, issued by Cyrus in 536 B.C., had to do with the rebuilding of the house of God (2 Chron. 36:22-23; Ezra 1:1f). The second, issued by Darius in 521 B.C., also related to the Temple (Ezra 6:3-8). The only decree about rebuilding Jerusalem itself was issued in the twentieth year of Artaxerxes, 445 B.C. (Neh. 2:1). What is more, we know the month. Anderson proceeds to assign a day:

> The Persian edict which restored the autonomy of Judah was issued in the Jewish month of Nisan. It may in fact have been dated the 1st of Nisan, but no other day being named, the prophetic period must be reckoned, according to a practice common with the Jews, from the Jewish New Year's Day. The seventy weeks are therefore to be computed from the 1st of Nisan, B.C. 445.[1]

THE SEVENTY WEEKS

PURPOSE: DESTINY

- to finish transgression
- to make an end of sin
- to make atonement for iniquity
- to bring in everlasting righteousness
- to seal up vision and prophecy (i.e., to fulfill it)
- to anoint the most holy place

CHRONOLOGY

69 SEVENS OF YEARS (360 days each = 173,880 days)		70TH WEEK
445 B.C. Decree to rebuild Jerusalem (Neh. 1-2; Dan. 9:25)	A.D. 32 Messiah cut off (Dan. 9:26)	A.D. ? Period of prophetic culmination

SUPPORT FOR THE TIME GAP

1. It is characteristic of Old Testament prophecy in general (e.g., Isa. 61; Luke 4).
2. The language of Daniel 9:26—"After the sixty-two weeks, the Messiah will be cut off."
3. History: "The people of the prince who is to come" (*not* the enemy prince himself) "will destroy the city and the sanctuary" (Dan. 9:26). This happened in A.D. 70 when a Roman army under Titus destroyed Jerusalem.
4. The New Testament (Matt. 24) expects that the events of the seventieth week are yet future.

Computing carefully, Sir Robert concluded that the sixty-nine weeks of years would have ended on April 6 of A.D. 32—"that fateful day on which the Lord Jesus rode into Jerusalem in fulfillment of the prophecy of Zechariah 9: 9; when, for the first and only occasion in all His earthly sojourn, He was acclaimed as 'Messiah the Prince, the King, the Son of David.' "[2]

History's end? We all know the events that followed on the heels of the triumphal entry. The proclaimed Messiah, Jesus, was in a few short days scorned by the very crowd that cheered him; he was "cut off" by execution. Out of the crucifixion came the resurrection, and with the resurrection came a new and previously undisclosed turn to history.

God's plan was proving to be more complex than had been imagined; the promised Deliverer now chose to put off the seventieth week, the culmination of history, so yet unborn generations would have the opportunity to benefit from His work on the cross. Forgiveness for the sinner, not only the establishment of the righteous Kingdom, was seen in a fresh and startling way to be God's concern.

And what of the seventieth week? What of the events detailed so carefully in Daniel 10 and 11, and referred to in Daniel 8 as destiny's climax? If we take Bible prophecy seriously . . . and these amazing fulfillments tell us we must . . . then we must also take seriously the Old Testament's portrait of the time of the end.

That time, that last seven years of history, is still ahead. We wait for it. And it rushes toward us. We cannot avoid a destiny in which the entire universe will take part. We must come to grips with destiny and its implications for us.

DIFFERING INTERPRETATIONS

Many who are thorough evangelicals would disagree vigorously with the suggestion that "taking Bible prophecy seriously" means accepting the viewpoint sketched above. What other viewpoints are held by those who also deeply trust and respect the Scriptures?

Approaches. One approach sees Old Testament prophecy as focused on the pre-Christian era. In this view, prophecies of regathering and return tell of the end of the Babylonian Exile, not the end of time. In a similar way, prophecy in the New Testament Book of Revelation seems to fit into church history rather than a short and final denouement at the return of Christ.

Another view stresses the poetic imagery that often marks prophetic passages. Since poetic language is by nature symbolic, some find it unnecessary to seek historic references or look for portraits of future events. The poetic encouragement, the expression of the transcendent sense of God's reality seems enough in itself.

Yet another view suggests that the prophecies present "spiritual" rather than "literal" views of the future. Thus the blessings of justice and prosperity under Messiah's reign are held to symbolize spiritual blessings experienced by the modern Christian. By this view, prophetic references to "Israel" refer not to the Jewish people but to the Church; Christians are the spiritual (though not physical) descendants of Abraham.

Perspectives. These various approaches to prophetic writings lead to differing pictures of the future. The individual who sees prophecy in the literal-historical framework generally tends to be premillennialist—that is, he believes Christ, the promised Messiah of the Old Testament, will establish a universal rule on earth when He returns. The premillennialist holds that the term *Israel* in Old Testament prophecy does refer to the Hebrew people (though often more narrowly to *believing* Jews) and not to the Church. In the premillennial view, the focus of much (if not most) of Old Testament prophecy is the end time rather than past history.

Those who see the prophecies as poetic or "spiritual" tend toward an amillennial view. That is, they believe that Old Testament prophecies were fulfilled in a spiritual sense either with the birth of Christ or in the immediate historical setting. Thus we should not expect a coming earthly rule by Messiah . . . the time of the end remains shrouded in mystery.

A choice. When we attempt a close examination of prophecy, we're forced to make a rather basic choice. Are we to understand these admittedly difficult and often figurative passages as having a literal-historical reference . . . or a spiritual-symbolic reference? It would be wrong to make either position a test of faith or fellowship; sincere believers are found on each side of this question. Yet to deal with the larger prophetic segments of the Old Testament, some orienting approach must be adopted.

For me personally, there seem to be many reasons for adopting the literal-historical standpoint. For that reason, these next chapters will reflect the premillennial position, and the passages of Scripture will be interpreted in that framework. Because interpretation varies so dramatically and completely between the two basic approaches, I have not made my usual attempt to outline "both sides." This certainly is not because of a contempt for the other approach or a lack of appreciation for the scholarship and commitment of those who take it. Rather, it seems best in this area to work with the framework of one basic position, exploring what the biblical data portrays when seen from that view.

What picture of the future does the "literal" understanding of prophecy provide? Let's investigate.

DANIEL 11-12

Much of Daniel's revelation of the future focuses on the seventieth week: the time of the end, when history is about to experience the divinely planned culmination. Yet again, sufficient details are given concerning past history to support the complete accuracy of Daniel's prediction and to give us confidence that the unfulfilled portion will be fulfilled with the same careful attention to detail.

Dan. 11:2-4. This describes again Alexander's rise

and the future division of his conquest to the four generals (see pp. 79-82).

Dan. 11:5-20. This predicts the struggles between the Ptolemys (Egypt; the South) and the Seleucids (the North), up until the time of Antiochus Epiphanes (ca. 175-164 B.C.). A study of the history of the intervening period shows just how literally and in what careful detail each dimension of this prophecy was fulfilled (see Wood's *Commentary on Daniel,* pp. 283-295).

Dan. 11:21-35. In this section the outrages of Antiochus, who launched a crusade against the Jewish faith, are predicted. As is common in Bible prophecy, the disaster launches the prophet beyond the prototype to the final enemy of God's people.

Dan. 11:36-45. In this section a new personality, like Antiochus in his drive to persecute God's people, is introduced. With supernatural aid, he wins great military victories, and exalts himself above every god. These prophecies fit the portrait given elsewhere of the Antichrist, a Satanic counterfeit of the promised ruler of righteousness. In spite of his great victories, "he will come to his end," (v. 45).

Dan. 12:1-4. Daniel's interpreter now goes on to speak of that period when the great enemy is unveiled, calling it a "time of distress such as never occurred since there was a nation until that time" (v. 1). In spite of the great tribulation by which those days are marked, deliverance comes to God's people; the period culminates in a bodily resurrection to "everlasting life" (v. 2). This is the first Scripture usage of this term—a common one in the New Testament. It is not, however, the first reference to a bodily resurrection (see Job 14:11-14; 19:25-27; Pss. 16:10; 49:15; Isa. 25:8; 26:19; Hos. 13:14). The resurrection of the ungodly is also spoken of here as a restoration "to disgrace and everlasting contempt" (v. 2).

Dan. 12:5-13. The final section of the book of Daniel seems to give a general chronology of this time of the end. Of particular note is the time period of 1,290 days specified in verse 11, 30 days beyond half of the last seven-year period of foretold history. Why the extra 30 days? The reason is uncertain, although some have suggested that they refer to the time of judgment for the nations mentioned by Jesus in Matthew 25:31-46 as following the great tribulation period.

Whatever the reason, if we take the pattern of fulfilled prophecy as our guide, we can be sure that these are literal days . . . and that when history overtakes prophecy, every detail will be seen and understood.

GOING DEEPER

to personalize

1. Read carefully the following passages of Daniel, which seem to focus on the seventieth week.

Dan. 2:33-45	Dan. 8:23-25	Dan. 11:36-45
Dan. 7:7-28	Dan. 9:27	Dan. 12:1-13

Make notes and try to determine the following:

- What time frame is in view, and how is it divided?
- Who are the chief characters in the final drama, and what are their parts?
- What events will take place in the final "week of years," and what can be told of their sequence?
- What will *follow* the "last week"?

2. Earlier the author noted that one key to interpreting prophecy is to fit each element to elements that are parallel or explanatory in other prophets' writings. Can you think of other passages that might relate to this time of the end?

3. Are you familiar with modern "prophets"? How do their "prophecies" compare and contrast with the Bible prophets? Particularly, what do you think is the implication of Deuteronomy 18:22 on evaluating the moderns?

to probe

1. How many fulfilled prophecies can you find in the Old Testament? (Use resource book if you choose; make a list of at least 100.)

2. For a major project, read J. Dwight Pentecost's book, *Things to Come* (Zondervan).

3. How might you use prophecy in (a) apologetics and (b) evangelism? Outline the possibilities in several pages.

1. Sir Robert Anderson, *The Coming Prince* (Grand Rapids: Kregel, 1954), p. 122.
2. Ibid.

8

Zechariah; Zephaniah

WORDS OF HOPE

WHILE DANIEL IN BABYLON was being given the "coming prince" prophecy of chapter 9, God was speaking to the people in Palestine by the prophet Zechariah. With his contemporary Haggai, Zechariah was used by God to stimulate the completion of the Temple. Even more, he brought words of hope to the Jews. Daniel warned of hundreds of years under a succession of Gentile world-rulers. Zechariah stressed the continuing concern of the Lord for His people and the final vindication of the Jewish hope. Messiah would come, and all the families of the earth would appear at Jerusalem to worship Him (Zech. 14:16).

As we continue our study of the Old Testament's springtime teachings, we find several values in Zechariah's fourteen chapters.

MAJOR THEMES REPEATED

When I taught Old Testament survey in the graduate school of Wheaton College, I used to give a pop quiz when we came to Zechariah. I asked my students to tell where they thought each of the following passages might be found.

> "When I scatter them among the peoples,
> They will remember Me in far countries,
> And they with their children will live and come back.
> I will bring them back from the land of Egypt,
> And gather them from Assyria:
> And I will bring them into the land. . . ."

* * *

> "And I will pour out on the house of David and on the inhabitants of Jerusalem the Spirit of grace and of supplication, so that they will look on Me whom they have pierced; and they will mourn for Him, as one mourns for an only son. . . ."

* * *

> "For I will gather all the nations against Jerusalem to battle, and the city will be captured, the houses plundered, the women ravished, and half of the city exiled, but the rest of the people will not be cut off from the city."

This was, of course, a "trick" quiz. Each of the passages above sounds very much like a theme from one of the prophets who lived and spoke in Israel or Judah before the Babylonian Captivity. These former prophets warned of a "scattering among nations" and a regathering to follow. They spoke of a change of heart associated with Messiah's coming. And they warned that enemy nations would assemble to battle and eventually overwhelm Jerusalem. We might think that these prophecies were at least in part fulfilled in the Babylonian Captivity. Nebuchadnezzar's armies besieged and finally destroyed Jerusalem, and the people were scattered through pagan lands. God acted to bring back a remnant from the nations where they were scattered; the Temple and city were rebuilt.

But what is so striking about these prophecies is that *each comes from Zechariah!* (10:9-10; 12:10; 14:2). Each was spoken *after* the exiles had, in large part, already returned. Zechariah, looking ahead, saw essentially the same future for Judah that the earlier prophets had seen. The interlude in Babylon had not fulfilled the warnings of an end time scattering and regathering or a great end time war against God's people and His Holy City.

This is an illustration of the law of double reference mentioned in chapter 6 (page 85). Zechariah's generation could see themselves in the portrait of judgment and restoration. But their generation was not to be the final generation; the ultimate fulfillment of the prophetic words still await the time of the end.

How do we explain the repetition of these themes and the up-and-down experience of Judah? We see the earth as a stage on which God has set a drama working out good and evil, the reconciliation of justice and love. The play has been written and the script placed in the actor's hands. We can see in the Scripture the amazing resolution planned by the Author. But God does not wait for the final production to demonstrate His genius. History contains a number of dress rehearsals. The Playwright's plan and the principles of reality that underlie the last act are woven into Judah's experience again and again so you and I can look back into history and see them illustrated. We can also look forward and understand what is to come.

And invite the actors to the after-celebration He has always had in mind for them!

The fact that warnings, principles, and promises found in the pre-exilic prophets are also found in the post-exilic prophets should not surprise us. *No experience up until the arrival of destiny exhausts the meaning of these prophets' words. The ultimate focus of prophecy is the time of the end.* That is why, in the final chapters of this study, we will draw from *all* the prophets to summarize the major themes of Old Testament prophecy.

FORMS OF PROPHECY

Zechariah also illustrates the variety of forms in which Old Testament prophecy came. Here we find vision and symbolic actions, principles expressed in institutions like the Temple, poetic expressions, prose statements, experiences reported, and oracles delivered in the certainty that "thus saith the Lord."

Visions. The first part of the Book of Zechariah (chaps. 1—6) reports eight visions given to the prophet. These are in most cases either interpreted or applied by an angelic messenger. The vision of the flying scroll (5:1-4) is typical. Here Zechariah reports seeing a flying book, or scroll, about thirty feet by fifteen feet in size! The angel explains: "This is the curse that is going forth over the face of the whole land; surely every one who steals will be purged away according to the writing on one side, and every one who swears will be purged away according to the writing on the other side. I will make it go forth," declares the Lord of hosts, "and it will enter the house of the thief and the house of the one who swears falsely by My name; and it will spend the night within that house and consume it with its timber and stones" (5:3-4).

Clearly God is acting in a distinct (and new?) way to administer justice severely and fairly. To what period of time does this vision apply? That's something we can't tell from the vision—but may be able to determine by looking at the broader context of the seven visions with which it is associated. Again, remember that the time factor in prophecy is normally open and relatively uncertain.

Symbolic acts. The prophets often take as a starting point an institution, person, or event from their own day as a launching pad for prophecy. Thus Joel, for instance, spoke of a great plague of locusts from his own time but used the devastation of the insects to portray the greater devastation that invading

SAMPLES OF PROPHETIC STYLE

A vision: the flying scroll	5:1-4
A symbolic act	6:9-15
A prophetic message	7:1—8:17
An oracle	chap. 14

hordes would work on the promised land in the end times.

In Zechariah 6:11 we hear the prophet told to make a crown of gold and silver and set it on the head of Joshua, the high priest. While there is direct reference to a role for Joshua in presiding over the restoration of the contemporary Temple, there is clearly a typical meaning as well, in which Joshua stands for another person yet to come. This is made clear immediately by the title the Branch, which was recognized by the Jews as a Messianic reference, and which is so used in Isaiah (4:2) and Jeremiah (23:5; 33:15).

What then is God saying about the Messiah through this incident and the words of coronation?

1. Messiah the Branch will build a future temple.
2. Messiah the Branch will rule as king.
3. Messiah the Branch will also have the office of priest, uniquely combining these two roles.
4. Messiah the Branch will bring together Jew and Gentile in common worship of the Lord.
5. Messiah the Branch will fulfill prophecy and validate the revealed Word.
6. Messiah the Branch will bring in full obedience to the voice of the Lord.

One of the striking aspects of this prophecy is the

apparent impossibility of its fulfillment! The coming King was to be of the tribe of Judah; the priests were from the line of Aaron. Thus it would be impossible for one man to be both priest and king; these two offices were kept forever separated. But when Jesus died, a new priesthood was established, not after the old Aaronic order but "after the order of Melchizedek" (see Hebrews 5). Thus the impossible *did* happen . . . and this "impossible prophecy" demonstrates anew the trustworthiness of the Word of God.

A prophetic message. In an extended section (chaps. 7—8) that seems to include four distinct themes or mini-messages, Zechariah answers a question raised by the men of Bethel. They have wondered if they need to keep on fasting on the anniversary of the destruction of Jerusalem now that the city has been restored.

Rebuked by the prophet—who asks whether their past fasting was out of sorrow for their own suffering or in repentance for their treatment of God ("These seventy years, was it actually for Me that you fasted?" 7: 5)—the people of Judah are reminded of God's requirements of holiness and then of His promise of restoration. This is meant to bring them hope in discouragement and fix their thoughts on the rejoicing that will be theirs when Messiah comes.

Again we see the emphasis on destiny. Present discouragement must always be evaluated in view of the certainty of ultimate blessing when God's promises to His people are finally fulfilled.

The oracles. The last part of Zechariah is clearly

focused on the culmination of God's plan. This is seen with great clarity in chapter 14, which describes the return of Messiah in great glory to consummate the divine program.

Many unusual details are introduced here, details sometimes repeated in other prophetic portraits.

1. There is to be a final siege of Jerusalem (14:1-2).

2. There is to be an appearance of the Lord on the earth, resulting in great topographical changes (14:3-8).

3. There will be a divine kingship established (14:9-11).

4. There will be punishment of Israel's enemies (14:12-15).

5. There will be a great conversion of the Gentile world to the Savior/King (14:16-19).

6. There will then be an experience of true holiness reflected in the purity of the worship offered the Lord (14:20-21).

It is clear from this quick review that not only are the prophetic forms many, but that each seems to lean forward. Each has in view, even when dealing with contemporary problems, the ultimate solution to human needs when Messiah comes to rule over the kingdoms of this world.

There is certainly no doubt or hesitation in the prophet's portrayal. There's a great day coming. A day of deliverance and restoration. Our present experience must be evaluated in view of what God is doing in our world and the destiny toward which history is swiftly carrying the universe itself.

THE STRUCTURE OF PROPHETIC BOOKS

So far, we've paid little attention to the structure of prophetic works in the Old Testament. We've noted that each prophet had a message for his contemporaries, and in an earlier study we viewed the prophetic ministry from that viewpoint. We've seen in this study that each prophet also has a message *for all men* concerning the direction and course of history.

Now we want to note a general characteristic of the way the Old Testament prophetic books are organized. Simply put, they generally (1) start with words of warning to the contemporary generation, (2) move on to announce coming judgment, (3) add an invitation to repent and be restored, and (4) conclude with a picture of the far future. This last section may focus on the final tragedies of that day, as God's righteousness finds its necessary expression in judgment on sin. Or the prophet may focus on the final glories of that day, when God brings in the peace and joy promised to His people. In almost every case, the last words of a prophet's writings are words of hope.

The Book of Zephaniah, a prophet who ministered just before the Captivity, illustrates that structure. Notice the pattern in the following outline on page 109.

Understanding this structure helps us quickly grasp the outline of most of the minor prophets' writings (those twelve shorter books of the prophets in the Old Testament, not including Jeremiah, Ezekiel, Isaiah, or Daniel). If we want a picture of

	ZEPHANIAH	
	Introduction	1:1
I.	Judgments on Judah	
	A. The judgments announced	1:2-9
	B. The judgments explained	1:10-18
II.	Invitation to repent	2:1-3
III.	Judgment on surrounding nations	2:4-15
IV.	More judgment on Judah	3:1-7
V.	Salvation: the Day of the Lord	3:9-18

the end time, we will look at the ending of a book . . . and then check carefully the descriptions of judgment to see if a near or distant expression of the judgment principle is in view.

In looking at the prophetic books in this way, we find that a number of themes are repeated over and over again. What we are to do in the final chapters of this springtime study is to isolate these themes . . . to examine them . . . and to see if we can discover more about the Bible's picture of what lies ahead.

GOING DEEPER

to personalize

1. Become more familiar with Bible prophecy by studying carefully the four passages from Zechariah indicated on the chart on page 105 (Zech. 5:1-4; 6:9-15; 7:1—8:17; and chapter 14).

2. Go back over these portions again, and jot down all the information you can find about what seems to you to describe the time of the end. (You may want to go over the material in Daniel relating to this time also.)

3. On page 111 you'll find a chart giving the broad outlines of the seventieth-week period of seven years. Transfer the information you gain from the prophets to that chart, trying to fit each bit of data into its most likely time period: the beginning, middle, or end of the period.

4. You'll want to add to this chart as we continue to develop insights into the prophesied future. Perhaps you'll want to make a larger, wall-sized chart to record your future discoveries.

5. Finally, read through Zephaniah, guided by the outline on page 109. If you wish to take notes, feel free, but don't worry at this point about adding to your prophetic chart.

to probe

1. Research one of the four passages you've studied (*personalize* 1) in two commentaries.

2. Outline the first six chapters of Zechariah, and see if you can determine the meaning of the eight night visions recorded there. Feel free to use a commentary if (but only if) you are unsatisfied with the understanding you can develop without one.

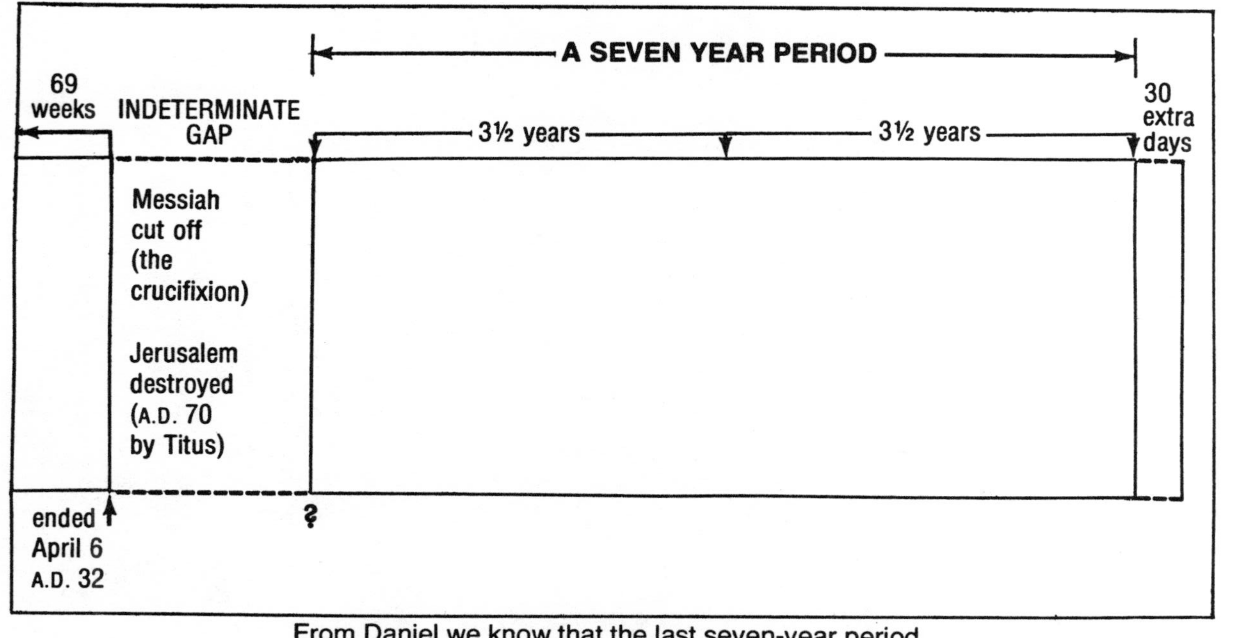

From Daniel we know that the last seven-year period of prophetic history is divided into two halves. What can you determine will happen then?

Part Three

THEMES OF THE END TIMES

9

Deuteronomy 28–30; selected prophets

A FINAL REGATHERING

ONE OF THE MOST COMMON themes of the Old Testament is that destiny will find the Jews in possession of Palestine. Hardly a popular theme in Arab countries, it is still one of the most basic and consistent teachings, with roots in far earlier days than those of the prophets.

THE COVENANTS

In an earlier book *(Let Day Begin)* we examined carefully a concept that is at the very root of Old Testament hope and the Jewish sense of identity. This is God's Covenant promise to Abraham, found in Genesis 12 and repeated in Genesis 15 and 17, and through Abraham to his descendants. That Covenant was God's unconditional oath that He would:

- *make Abraham a great nation* (well fulfilled, as Abraham is the progenitor of Jew and Arab alike!)

- *bless Abraham* (well fulfilled, as God counted Abraham's faith for righteousness)
- *make Abraham's name great* (well fulfilled, as Jew, Moslem, and Christian all look to Abraham and honor him as a founder of their faiths)
- *bless those who treat Abraham's people well and curse those who do not* (well fulfilled in history, even as recent as Nazi and British betrayals of God's Old Testament people)
- *bless all the families of the world through Abraham* (well fulfilled in Jesus, the Savior, who is a Jew) and finally
- *give Abraham and his descendants the land of Palestine* (still *un*fulfilled in its defined extent)

The land "from the river of Egypt as far as the great river, the river Euphrates" (Gen. 15:18) has in historic times been *partially occupied* by the Hebrew peoples, but in its defined extent it has never yet been theirs.

As the centuries passed, the original Covenant with Abraham was further defined in additional covenants. The Davidic Covenant promised that a descendant of David's would rule: "Your throne shall be established for ever" (1 Sam. 7:16). Permanent, endless rule over Israel's Promised Land was guaranteed to one from David's family.

Again centuries passed. First the northern tribes were torn away from the land and taken to captivity (722 B.C.); then Judah was led to Babylon by a later conqueror (586 B.C.). Did this mean the old promises were set aside? That God's earlier promises had been withdrawn because of His people's sin?

To avoid this misunderstanding, a New Covenant was announced through the prophet Jeremiah. God had not given up on the Jews, nor had He gone back on His oath.

> "Restrain your voice from weeping,
> And your eyes from tears"
> . . . declares the Lord,
> "And they shall return from the land of the enemy,
> And there is hope for your future," declares the Lord,
> "And your children shall return to their own territory."
>
> *Jeremiah 31:16-17*

In this New Covenant promise God announced His intention of changing the hearts of His people in a great national conversion:

> "I will put My law within them, and on their heart I will write it; and I will be their God, and they shall be My people. And they shall not teach again, each man his neighbor and each man his brother, saying, 'Know the Lord,' for they shall all know Me, from the least of them to the greatest of them," declares the Lord, "for I will forgive their iniquity, and their sin I will remember no more."
>
> *Jeremiah 31:33-34*

The twisted tendency to sin and turn away from God, no matter how great the experience of His love, will be removed. A new, responsive heart will be given. Only then will the land become theirs to possess forever.

Law. Of all the covenants in the Old Testament, the Covenant of Law is distinct. Given first in external form, written on stone tablets at Sinai, God's rules for holy living were to be replaced by a New Covenant through which righteousness would be written within the believer's personality. This is one distinctive of the Law Covenant: it alone is to be replaced.

Another distinctive is that the Law Covenant is a conditional covenant. The Law does not speak of God's oath or promise. It is instead a contract between God and Israel. If Israel obeys, God will bless. If not, God will act in judgment.

A final distinctive of the Mosaic Law is that it focuses on the present experience of each generation of Jews. It does *not* have the end times in view. If a given generation obeys, God will give them the blessings held in store for the final generation at the end of time when His promises are kept. Thus Israel and Judah were torn from the land when their sin demanded judgment . . . and when a new generation turned to God (as under the leadership of Zerubbabel described by Ezra), the people were blessed.

DISTINCTIVES OF THE MOSAIC LAW COVENANT

It alone . . .

. . . was to be replaced
. . . was conditional (a contract, not an oath)
. . . was focused on the present time, not the future.

This principle of removal from the land for sin, and restoration when repentance came, is stated first not in the works of the prophets but in the books of Moses, in Deuteronomy.

"Now it shall be, if you will diligently obey the Lord your God, being careful to do all His commandments which I command you today, the Lord your God will set you high above all the nations of the earth. And all these blessings shall come upon you and overtake you, if you will obey the Lord your God.

" . . . And the Lord shall make you the head and not the tail, and you only shall be above, and you shall not be underneath, if you will listen to the commandments of the Lord your God, which I charge you today, to observe them carefully, and do not turn aside from any of the words which I command you today, to the right or to the left, to go after other gods to serve them.

"But it shall come about, if you will not obey the Lord your God, to observe to do all His commandments and His statutes which I charge you today, that all these curses shall come upon you and overtake you.

" . . . The Lord will cause you to be defeated before your enemies.

" . . . The Lord will bring you and your king whom you shall set over you to a nation which neither you nor your fathers have known, and there you shall serve other gods, wood and stone. And you shall become a horror, a proverb, and a taunt among all the people where the Lord will drive you.

"... So all these curses shall come on you and pursue you and overtake you until you are destroyed, because you would not obey the Lord your God by keeping His commandments and His statutes which He commanded you. And they shall become a sign and a wonder on you and your descendants forever.

Deuteronomy 28:1-2, 13-15, 25, 36-37, 45-46

This outline of history ahead . . . striking in its preview of what *did* happen to God's people... is not so much prophecy as promise. It is a statement of principles to govern God's dealings with his people; it is an exhortation to Israel to choose life and good, not death and evil. Yet with the warning came another kind of promise as well. Whatever might happen to a particular generation, God would still remain true to His Abrahamic oath.

"So it shall become when all of these things have come upon you, the blessing and the curse which I have set before you, and you call them to mind in all the nations where the Lord your God has banished you, and you return to the Lord your God and obey Him with all your heart and soul according to all that I command you today, you and your sons, then the Lord your God will restore you from captivity, and have compassion on you, and will gather you again from all the peoples where the Lord your God has scattered you. If your outcasts are at the ends of the earth, from there the Lord your God will gather you, and from there He will bring you back. And the Lord your God will bring you into the land which your fathers possessed, and you shall possess it; and He will prosper you and multiply you more than your fathers. Moreover the Lord your God will circumcise your heart and the heart of your descendants, to love the Lord your God with all your heart and with all your soul, in order that you may live.

Deuteronomy 30:1-6

WHEN?

When has all this been fulfilled? Or is it yet to be?

The answer is complex, for this scattering and regathering has happened *often* . . . and will be fulfilled *finally*.

Often. Reading Old Testament history, we can't help being impressed by the fact that the Deuteronomy picture of apostasy, judgment, repentance, and restoration has been repeated over and over again. We saw it in the experience of Israel in the wilderness; the disobedient generation died, the responsive generation went on to conquest. The days of the judges were marked by repeated cycles of what one commentator has labeled "sin, servitude, supplication, salvation, and silence."

Under godly David, Israel's kingdom expanded, and much (but not all) of the Promised Land was occupied by the Israelites. Then came the division of the kingdom, with the history of Israel and then

Judah marked by decline and ultimately captivity. Even brief but brilliant revivals under Judah's godly kings did not reverse the downhill trend.

Then came the Captivity, and afterward the return. Back in the land again, however, we've seen how the later generations again fell away from God, until in the time of Malachi the people were hardened and unresponsive.

Looking beyond Old Testament times, we see Israel given the ultimate opportunity in the person of the promised Messiah-King, Jesus. Rejection of Him led to yet another scattering, and for nearly two thousand years the Jewish people had no homeland at all in Palestine.

History itself gives living testimony to the complete accuracy of the Word of God. Of all the peoples the world has known, only the Jews have maintained their identity as a people even when torn away for centuries from geographical and national roots. Only with the Jews has this pattern of judgment and restoration—apostasy, scattering, and regathering—held true.

In one sense, the picture of scattering and regathering we see in Scripture *has been* fulfilled . . . and often!

Finally. Yet it's clear that the statement in Deuteronomy has a final sense. One regathering is associated with the Lord "circumcising the heart" (Deut. 30: 6) of the Jews so they and their offspring will love Him, and no further scattering will follow. This prophetic promise finds clearer expression in Jeremiah's announcement of a New Covenant to be

THE NEW COVENANT

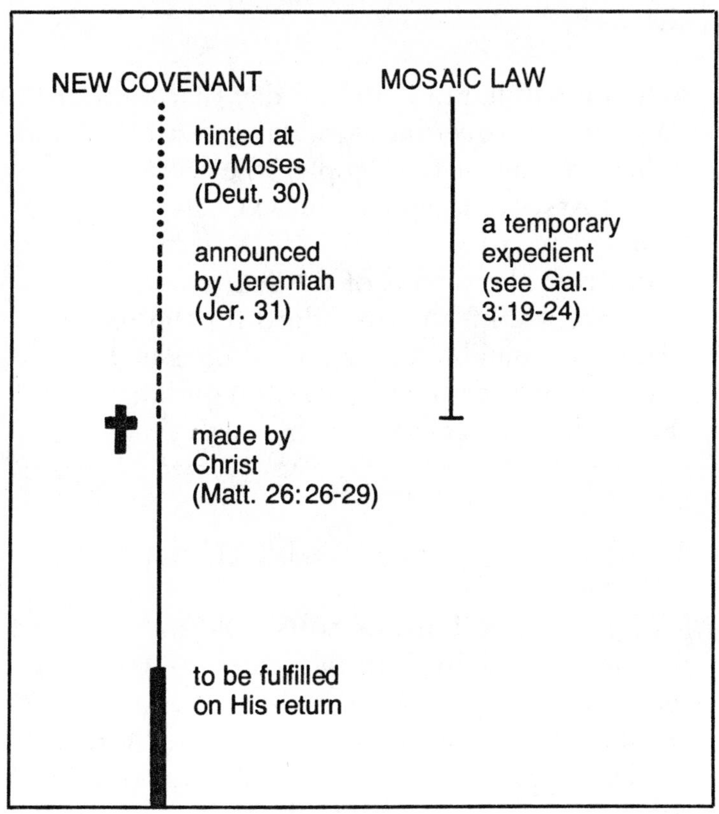

made with the house of Israel in a day future to his own. The keeping of that New Covenant is associated with the final regathering of the Jews to Palestine.

One of the most striking aspects of Old Testament prophecy is the picture of the final regathering projected by both the pre-exilic and post-exilic prophets. Isaiah prophesied long before the first exile:

> Then it will happen on that day that the Lord
> Will again recover the second time with His hand
> The remnant of His people, who will remain,
> From Assyria, Egypt, Pathros, Cush, Elam, Shinar, Hamath,
> And from the islands of the sea.
> And He will lift up a standard for the nations,
> And will assemble the banished ones of Israel,
> And will gather the dispersed of Judah
> From the four corners of the earth.
>
> *Isaiah 11:11, 12*

And after the captives returned, Zechariah wrote . . .

> "Thus says the Lord of hosts, 'Old men and old women will again sit in the streets of Jerusalem, each man with his staff in his hand because of age. And the streets of the city shall be filled with boys and girls playing in its streets.' Thus says the Lord of hosts, 'If it is too difficult in the sight of the remnant of this people in those days, will it also be too difficult in My sight?' declares the Lord of hosts. Thus says the Lord of hosts, 'Behold, I am going to save My people from the land of the east and from the land of the west; and I will bring them back, and they will live in the midst of Jerusalem, and they will be My people and I will be their God in truth and righteousness.' "
>
> *Zechariah 8:4-8*

NOW?

For some nineteen hundred years of the Christian era (that unexpected gap between Daniel's sixty-ninth and seventieth week), the Jewish people had no national homeland. Then, in 1948, a Jewish state was established. Struggling in constant warfare with Arab neighbors bent on its destruction, the young nation has been victorious in each outbreak of fighting and has constantly expanded its holdings. While still far from the borders spoken of in the Old Testament, the Jewish return to the homeland is taking place for the first time in centuries.

Is *this* part of the fulfillment? Does this indicate that the final regathering . . . the final week of years . . . is drawing near?

There is no way to give a time schedule for that final week. It might begin tomorrow . . . or decades from now. Yet there is one prophecy of return that sheds amazing light on contemporary events. It is recorded by Ezekiel in the thirty-seventh chapter of his book.

Ezekiel tells of being taken by the Spirit of the Lord to a valley full of very dry bones of long dead animals. Ezekiel is asked, "Can these bones live?" Uncertain, the prophet is told to command the bones to speak in the name of the Lord and call the dead to life . . . and he watches as first the bones stir and fit themselves together, then are covered by growing sinews, flesh and skin, and then stand whole again to receive the breath of life.

Finally, the meaning of the vision is explained to the prophet.

"These bones are the whole house of Israel; behold, they say, 'Our bones are dried up, and our hope has perished. We are completely cut off.' Therefore prophesy, and say to them, 'Thus says the Lord God, "Behold, I will open your graves and cause you to come up out of your graves, My people; and I will bring you into the land of Israel. Then you will know that I am the Lord, when I have opened your graves and caused you to come up out of your graves, My people. And I will put My spirit within you, and you will come to life, and I will place you on your own land. Then you will know that I, the Lord, have spoken and done it," declares the Lord.' "

Ezekiel 37:11-14

For many, this striking vision seems to portray modern Israel. Taken from their graves among the Gentile nations, with many rescued from the very ovens of Nazi oppression, the dry bones gathered. Increasingly in the past decades, sinews and flesh and skin have been added—a people brought together into something new and whole. And yet the nation Israel is without spiritual life; they have not recognized Jesus as Messiah.

How soon will the prophecy be completed?

We have no way of knowing.

But even today, as we look across the ocean toward the Mediterranean world, many are convinced that we can see the shape of springtime and sense destiny in the air.

GOING DEEPER

to personalize

1. Explore the key prophetic passages that sketch the pattern of scattering and that promise return. Begin with Deuteronomy 28—30, and jot down everything related to this theme you observe.

2. Continue to examine prophecies about return. Here is a list from the writings of the prophets. Read them, and jot down your observations. For instance, is the final return naturally or supernaturally achieved? Where are the people of the return to be found? How is this like or unlike the return described in Ezra and Nehemiah? In other words, *think carefully* about each passage, and note down details.

The passages:

Isaiah 11:11-12; 14:1-3; 27:12-13; 43:1-8; 49:16; 66:20-22
Jeremiah 16:14-16; 23:3-8; 30:10-11; 31:8, 31-37
Ezekiel 11:17-21; 20:33-38; 34:11-16; 39:25-29
Hosea 1:10-11
Joel 3:17-21
Amos 9:11-15
Micah 4:4-7
Zephaniah 3:14-20
Zechariah 8:4-8

3. Study carefully the vision of the dry bones (Ezek. 37). What do *you* think? Might this describe Israel's history since 1948?

to probe

1. Add any data you wish to your chart (page 111).
2. Research the history of Israel from 1948 to the present. Write a brief review of that history, and discuss its relationship to Old Testament prophecies outlined above (*personalize* 2, 3).

10

selected prophets

GREAT TRIBULATION

OF ALL THE THEMES associated with the final seven years of destiny, probably none draws quite so much attention as the warning of a great tribulation. We find this warning often in the Old Testament, like these words of Amos to those of his day who were eager for the coming of destiny's promised glory:

> Alas, you who are long for the day of the Lord,
> For what purpose will the day of the Lord be to you?
> It will be darkness and not light;
> As when a man flees from a lion,
> And a bear meets him,
> Or goes home, leans his hand against the wall,
> And a snake bites him.
> Will not the day of the Lord be darkness instead of light,
> Even gloom with no brightness in it?
>
> *Amos 5:18-20*

A variety of events are included in this "day." For instance, Zechariah includes the following:

> Behold, a day is coming for the Lord when the spoil taken from you will be divided among you. For I will gather all the nations against Jerusalem to battle, and the city will be captured, the house plundered, the women ravished, and half of the city exiled, but the rest of the people will not be cut off from the city. Then the Lord will go forth and fight against those nations as when He fights on the day of battle. And in that day His feet will stand on the Mount of Olives, which is in front of Jerusalem on the east; and the Mount of Olives will be split in its middle from east to west by a very large valley, so that half of the mountain will move toward the north, and the other half toward the south.
>
> *Zechariah 14:1-4*

Clearly an extended time span is implied: time enough for an invasion and conquest of Jerusalem; time enough for the city to be emptied of half its inhabitants; time enough for the Lord to come in person to battle against the nations in rebellion; time enough for the final battle to be concluded and great geographic changes to be made in Palestine when "His feet will stand on the Mount of Olives" (14:4).

What is important to note here is that the *time of the end* sketched in the Old Testament is not a single event but *a series of events* taking place over a period of time. Thus, too, what Christians call the Second

Coming of Christ, if it has any relationship at all to the Old Testament picture of the future (see chapter 13), is not a solitary or single event. Just as the events of Jesus' first coming took place over thirty-some years, so also the events associated with the Second Coming are complex and involve an extended period of time.

All of us have a tendency to oversimplify, to stress one aspect of an idea at the expense of others. Often young people looking forward to marriage see only its promised joys . . . and completely overlook the conflicts and struggles to adjust that will be part of married life. One aspect of the relationship seems to dominate their thinking, and the total picture is distorted or lost.

This is what was happening in Amos's day. The people of Israel—the northern, apostate tribes—were delighted with those Old Testament teachings of a coming Kingdom and the glory they thought they would share as the people of the King. What they forgot was that the same Old Testament tells about a time of trouble to precede the glory. The last seven years of Daniel's prophecy (a prophecy not yet given in Amos's day) were to be a time of terrible purification for God's people. Many would suffer and die: only a remnant would be saved.

And so Amos warns the men and women of his day who were eager for the prize but who had shown themselves unwilling to pay the price of obedience to God:

Don't be so eager for destiny.

Destiny's dawn is shrouded in darkness. The coming of springtime will be marked by the most cruel blast of winter ever known.

THE DAY OF THE LORD

The Day of the Lord (also called "that day," "the day," or "the great day") is a much-repeated theme in both Old and New Testaments. The phrase *Day of the Lord* is found in the King James Version renditions of Isaiah 2:12; 13:6, 9; Ezekiel 13:5; 30:3; Joel 1:15; 2:1, 11, 31; 3:14; Amos 5:18, 20; Obadiah 15; Zephaniah 1:7, 14; Zechariah 14:1; Malachi 4:5. It is also found in Acts 2:20; 1 Thessalonians 5:2; 2 Thessalonians 2:2; 2 Peter 3:10. The other terms ("that day," etc.,) recur more than seventy-five times in the Old Testament.

In an extended passage, Dwight Pentecost gives his forecast of the Day of the Lord:

> It will include the prophesied events of the tribulation period, such as: the federation of states into a Roman Empire (Dan. 2 and 7); the rise of the political ruler of this empire, who makes a covenant with Israel (Dan. 9:27; Rev. 13:1-10); the formulation of a false religious system under the false prophet (Rev. 13:11-18); the pouring out of the judgments under the seals (Rev. 6); the separation of the 144,000 witnesses (Rev. 7); the trumpet judgments (Rev. 8—11); the rise of God's witnesses (Rev. 11); the persecution of Israel (Rev. 12); the pouring out of the bowl judgments (Rev. 16); the events of the campaign of Armageddon (Ezek. 38 and 39; Rev. 16:16; 19:17-21); the proclamation of the gospel of the kingdom (Matt. 14:14). It will also

> include the prophesied events connected with the second advent, such as: the return of the Lord (Matt. 24:14); the resurrection of Old Testament and tribulation saints (John 6:39-40; Rev. 20:4); the destruction of the Beast and all his armies and the False Prophet and his followers in the Beast worship (Rev. 19:11-21); the judgment on the nations (Matthew 25:31-46); the regathering of Israel (Ezek. 37:1-14); the judgment on living Israel (Ezek. 20:33-38); the restoration of Israel to the land (Amos 9:15); the binding of Satan (Rev. 20:2-3). Further it will include all the events of the millennial age, with the final revolt of Satan (Rev. 20:7-10); the great white throne judgment (Rev. 20:11-15); and the purging of earth (2 Pet. 3:10-13). These, and many related subjects, must be studied [if we are to understand "that day"].[1]

Several things about Pentecost's view should be noted.

First, it integrates Old and New Testament teachings. He assumes that the Old Testament picture of springtime is essentially accurate and that the New Testament revelation may add to our understanding but will not change the earlier revelation.

Second, it involves a complex sequence of events. Nowhere in Scripture is this particular sequence given to us. Dr. Pentecost's way of fitting the prophesied events together may well be accurate. But we cannot be sure. *How* the events fit into the period is gathered from careful deduction; our deductions may be wrong.

Third, many themes in Scripture are associated with the time of the end. God is going to bring all things together in Christ when the end comes; that ending is more complex and involved than we can know. So we need to avoid fastening on a single passage or end time theme and treating it as if it were the whole story. We need to recognize our own limitations in understanding, realizing that God has not given us either a time schedule or an agenda in prophecy. What He has given us is a bold picture of the culmination of all things, a picture drawn with a sweeping brush on the canvas of the future. From where we stand, the details may not yet be clear, but we *can* make out those clear and vibrant colors with which God has painted His picture of world's end. It is those major themes—the vivid colors—we should keep in mind.

What we learn about God and about ourselves from the big picture is what is important in our study of Old Testament prophecy. Arguments over sequence and detail are not!

Purified. The picture of the Day of the Lord and the tribulation period is a picture of a purposeful judgment. It is a terrible time, with the earth wasted and emptied, its inhabitants desolate. It is a time of God's indignation and punishment, of trouble and gloom and darkness when His wrath comes to rest on mankind (see Deut. 4:30-31; Isa. 2:19; 24:1, 3, 6; 24:19-21; 26:20-21; Jer. 30:7; Dan. 9:27; 12:1; Joel 1:15; 2:1-2; Amos 5:18-20; Zeph. 1:14-15, 18).

It is clear from Scripture that this is the day of *God's* wrath: He Himself is the one terrorizing the earth and bringing judgment upon it. But *whom* is He judging, and why does judgment take this form?

In Deuteronomy, the seedbed passage of chapters 28—30 indicates that Israel is the focus of history. Nations around her will rise and fall with her fortunes; when the need for judgment comes, enemy peoples will be the instruments God uses to discipline His own. Daniel made it clear that his prophecy concerning the seventieth week as well as the other sixty-nine focuses on Israel: "Seventy weeks have been decreed *for your people and your holy city* . . ." (9: 24). The Jewish emphasis is further seen in passages such as Deut. 4: 30; Jer. 30: 7; Ezek. 20: 37; Dan. 12: 1-2, 7; etc.

At the same time Gentile men and nations are to experience judgment, for the tribulation is a worldwide experience. As Jeremiah prophetically describes it,

> Behold, evil is going forth
> From nation to nation,
> And a great storm is being stirred up
> From the remotest parts of the earth.
> And those slain by the Lord on that day shall be from one end of the earth to the other. They shall not be lamented, gathered, or buried . . .
>
> *Jeremiah 25:32-33*

Yet with all the stunning terror of the tribulation time, it is clear that even judgments are designed to lead to deliverance.

> Alas! for that day is great,
> There is none like it;

And it is the time of Jacob's distress,
But he will be saved from it.

Jeremiah 30:7

And I shall make you pass under the rod, and I shall bring you into the bond of the covenant; and I shall purge from you the rebels. . . .

Ezekiel 20:37-38

"And it will come about in all the land,"
Declares the Lord,
"That two parts in it will be cut off and perish;
But the third will be left in it.
And I will bring the third part through the fire,
Refine them as silver is refined,
And test them as gold is tested.
They will call on My name,
And I will answer them;
I will say, 'They are My people,
And they will say, 'The Lord is my God.' "

Zechariah 13:8-9

This salvation purpose extends to the Gentiles as well as the Jews. For out of that great tribulation time, in which a terrible toll of lives will be taken, comes a day of deliverance that extends to all nations.

Now it will come about that
In the last days,
The mountain of the house of the Lord
Will be established as the chief of the mountains,

And will be raised above the hills;
And all nations will stream to it.

Isaiah 2:1-2

And nations will come to your light,
And kings to the brightness of your rising.

Isaiah 60:3

The time of trouble leads to this consummation and involves personal cleansing (see also Rev. 7:9; 14:4) and preparation for national conversion of Israel (Ezek. 10:37-38; Zech. 13:1, 8-9). This picture of that day leads us to the Old Testament doctrine of the remnant.

The remnant. A survey of Israel's history indicates how often God found it necessary to give His people a new start following judgment. Even before the call of Abraham, the story of Noah expresses this principle. Humanity had turned away from God (Gen. 6—9); He chose a single responsive man and his family to bring through the flood of judgment.

On the journey out of Egypt, the bodies of the disobedient were left behind as they died during the wilderness wanderings. Only Joshua and Caleb of the original group lived to enter the Promised Land with the new generation.

In the time of the division of the kingdom, when the false worship system was set up in Israel by Jeroboam I, true believers slipped across the border to settle in Judah, where God might be worshiped according to the Law. Those who remained were carried away in 722 B.C. by Sargon into captivity.

As the people of Judah became confirmed in their sin, God sent the Babylonians, and Judah too went away into exile. Many were killed in the siege and battle, but a remnant remained in captivity. Later, an even smaller remnant "whose spirit God had stirred" (Ezra 1:5) left the land of their exile to return to Palestine.

In each of these situations, we see God preserving a portion of His people, and, through judgment on the nation, purifying those who survive.

An examination of the prophets makes it clear that the theme of the remnant who survive the great tribulation, and who are turned to God by it, and who enter the promised time of blessing, is a major theme of prophecy related to this period (see Isa. 1:9; 4:3-4; 6:12-13; 10:21; 26:20; 51:1; 65:13-14; Jer. 15:11; 33:25-26; 44:28; Ezek. 14:22; 20:34-38; 37:21-22; Hos. 3:5; Amos 9:11-15; Zech. 13:8-9; Mal. 3:16-17).

However tragic and terrible the opening phases of the Day of the Lord will be, God will bring many of His people through the judgments and welcome them to the full enjoyment of springtime.

FOR US?

Whenever Christians look at this great and terrible tribulation coming on the world, the question is asked: "Are *we* going to experience it too?" Certainly Jesus, when asked about the end of the age by His disciples, made it clear that the seventieth week and its troubles still lay ahead . . . and gave this teaching:

> When you see the abomination of desolation which was spoken of through Daniel the prophet [*in chapters 9:27; 11:31; 12:11; and related specifically to the seventieth week*], standing in the holy place (let the reader understand), then let those who are in Judea flee to the mountains; let him who is on the housetop not go down to get the things out that are in his house; and let him who is in the field not turn back to get his cloak. . . . For then there will be a great tribulation, such as has not occurred since the beginning of the world until now, nor ever shall. And unless those days had been cut short, no life would have been saved; but for the sake of the elect those days shall be cut short.
>
> *Matthew 24:15-22*

But shortly after Jesus uttered these words, Daniel's sixty-ninth week came to a close; Messiah *was* cut off, just as the prophet had foretold. An unexpected, extended period of time intervened; it has now stretched across centuries. One day, and perhaps one day soon, the countdown Daniel began so long ago—that God placed on "hold" when Jesus died—will begin again. We do know from Jesus' words in Matthew that the tribulation will still focus on Palestine. We know that once again there will be a holy place, a Temple, in Jerusalem. But whether we will be present for the tribulation of those days . . . there is debate.

In the New Testament we're told that one part of that complex plan for the end involves what is called the "Rapture" of the Church. Jesus in His coming will be met in the air by believers of this age (1 Thess. 4). But we are not certain when this will take place. Many say before the tribulation (thus, the label *pre-tribulationists);* others say in the middle of the tribulation period, about 3½ years into the 7-year period *(midtribulationists);* others say after the tribulation *(posttribulationists).* Each argue from Scripture . . . but each relies on deduction to fit events together in a sequence that is not itself revealed.

Because of that, we hesitate to argue dogmatically for any one of these positions. What we can say with certainty is this: there is portrayed over and over again in the Old Testament a specific time of the end, and this time begins with a worldwide experience of tribulation and terror never known on earth before. That tribulation is the final purifying; a remnant of those who are responsive to God will not only survive but will joyfully welcome springtime.

GOING DEEPER

to personalize

1. To get a sense of the impact of the Day of the Lord and its judgment aspects, look up and read at least one of the following two sets of passages. Take notes on what you see as significant, especially anything that might help you add to your chart on page 111.

Day of the Lord: Isa. 2:12; 13:6, 9; Ezek. 13:5; 30:3; Joel 1:15; 2:1, 11, 31; 3:14; Amos 5:18-20; Obadiah 15; Zeph. 1:7, 14; Zech. 14:1; Mal. 4:5.

Tribulation: Deut. 4:30-31; Isa. 2:19; 24:1, 3, 6;

24:19-21; 26:20-21; Jer. 30:7; Dan. 9:27; 12:1; Joel 1:15; 2:1-2; Amos 5:18-20; Zeph. 1:14-15, 18.

2. The text noted that there seems to be no complete *sequential* listing of the events of the Day of the Lord in the Old Testament. Probably the closest to a sequence is provided in Zechariah 10—14. Read this passage carefully, (a) list the *major events* you see there, and (b) watch for hints concerning sequence.

3. After reading the passages, how do you feel about the tribulation period? How would you feel about living through it? Why? How might the Jew of Old Testament days have felt about the coming tribulation?

to probe

1. Look up several books on prophecy, seeking those that take different positions on the Rapture. List their arguments for each position. Then argue from the *Old Testament alone* in support of the position you feel is most likely to be correct.

1. J. Dwight Pentecost, *Things to Come* (Grand Rapids: Zondervan, 1958), p. 231.

11

selected prophets

THE CAST OF CHARACTERS

IT IS AMAZING that God's Old Testament people looked forward so eagerly to Messiah and to His glorious Kingdom. Reading both the Old and New Testament documents, the impression grows that most of the Jewish people saw only the final result of Daniel's seventieth week; they were blind to or skipped quickly over the description of the week itself. The tribulation events seemed unreal to them, while the vision of national power and exaltation over their Gentile enemies captured their imaginations.

Yet the end time is portrayed so strongly as a time of "darkness and not light" that woe is pronounced on those who, in spite of their sins, eagerly expect it (Amos 5:18). A far more appropriate attitude is reflected in Habakkuk, who saw the meaning of the coming judgment just before the Babylonians struck Judah:

> I heard and my inward parts trembled;
> At the sound my lips quivered.

Decay enters my bones,
And in my place I tremble.
Because I must wait quietly for the day of distress.
Habakkuk 3:16

Shaken by the vision of impending judgment, Habakkuk still is strengthened by his personal trust in God.

Yet I will exult in the Lord,
I will rejoice in the God of my salvation.
The Lord God is my strength,
And He has made my feet like hinds' feet,
And makes me walk on my high places.
Habakkuk 3:18-19

The more clearly drawn we see the time of the end in Scripture, the more seriously we must view it. And the more our faith and joy must be rooted in the Lord. This is particularly true when we turn to the Old Testament to meet the cast of characters who take leading roles during the final times.

WORLD POWERS

An extensive outline of the political structure of the end times in Scripture reveals no one-world government but rather several power blocs.

West. In the West, a power bloc described in Daniel 2:41-42; 7:7f; and 8:9-26 emerges. This is the final expression of the fourth empire of Daniel's visions, the Roman. In final form it seems to be a coalition of ten states, some weak and some strong, that gradually come under the power of an individual who is Satan's counterfeit of the Messiah. This Western power, generally conceded to be the territory held by the ancient Roman Empire of Jesus' day, is central in the Old Testament picture of the end.

North. To the north the Old Testament portrays a second great confederacy, described in Ezekiel 38:1—39:25; Daniel 11:40; Joel 2:1-17; Isaiah 30:31-33; and other passages. The allied nations are identified as Gog, Magog, Rosh, Meshech, and Tubal. Much study has been given to identifying these peoples and lands, and there is an agreement that the confederacy includes Russia, Iran, certain Arab states, Easy Germany, and some Asian peoples.

East. There is additional mention, in Revelation 16:12 in the New Testament, of a coalition of Asian powers who invade Palestine in a confrontation with the head of the revived Roman Empire.

South. Finally, there is another power, mentioned in Daniel 11:40, which is Egyptian or North African. This power is the first to be confronted by the Western bloc and is destroyed by it.

What is of course striking about this political geography is its resemblance to today's world situation. A divided Germany (the first Roman Empire did not include *all* of Germany, but approximately the West Germany of today!), a Common Market that might become a confederacy or "United States of Europe" (always the goal of some of its founders), the rise of Russia and the gathering of its present satellites—all these make reading Old Testament prophecy seem much like reading today's newspaper.

For the first time in some nineteen centuries, the political shape of our world fits the Old Testament description of the distribution of power at the time of the end.

THE ANTICHRIST

The Old Testament describes in great detail the leader of the Western powers. His character and his activities are presented in Ezekiel 28:1-10 and Daniel 7:7-8, 20-26; 8:23-25; 9:26-27; 11:36-45 as well as in New Testament passages such as 2 Thessalonians 2:3-10 and Revelation 13:1-10.

From these passages Dwight Pentecost has drawn together twenty-nine items that sum up the Antichrist's life and impact on the time of the end. In looking at this extended quote from Pentecost's book *Things to Come,* notice again the sequence suggested, which may or may not be correct in detail but shows an interrelationship between elements of the Old Testament revelation and the New.

> (1) He will appear on the scene in the "latter times" of Israel's history (Dan. 8:23). (2) He will not appear until the Day of the Lord has begun (2 Thess. 2:3). (3) His manifestation is being hindered by the Restrainer (2 Thess. 2:6-7). (4) This appearance will be preceded by a departure (2 Thess. 2:3), which may be interpreted either as a departure from the faith or a departure of

the saints to be with the Lord (2 Thess. 2:1). (5) He is a Gentile, since he arises from the sea (Rev. 13:1) and since the sea depicts the Gentile nations (Rev. 17:15), he must be of Gentile origin. (6) He rises from the Roman empire, since he is a ruler of the people who destroyed Jerusalem (Dan. 9:26). (7) He is the head of the last form of Gentile world dominion, for he is like a leopard, a bear, and a lion (Rev. 13:2). (Cf. Daniel 7:7-8, 20, 24; Rev. 17:9-11). As such he is a political leader. The seven heads and ten horns (Rev. 13:1; 17:12) are federated under his authority. (8) His influence is world wide, for he rules over all nations (Rev. 13:8). This influence comes through the alliance which he makes with other nations (Dan. 8:24; Rev. 17:12). (9) He has eliminated three rulers in his rise to power (Dan. 7:8, 24). One of the kingdoms over which he has authority has been revived, for one of the heads, representing a kingdom, or king (Rev. 17:10), has been healed (Rev. 13:3). (10) His rise comes through his peace program (Dan. 8:25). (11) He personally is marked by his intelligence and persuasiveness (Dan. 7:8, 20; 8:23) and also by his subtlety and craft (Ezek. 28:5), so that his position over the nations is by their own consent (Rev. 17:13). (12) He rules over the nations in his federation with absolute authority (Dan. 11:36), where he is depicted as doing his own will. This authority is manifested through the change in laws and customs (Dan. 7:25). (13) His chief interest is in might and power (Dan. 11:38). (14) As the head of the federated empire he makes a seven year covenant with Israel (Dan. 9:27), which is broken after three and one half years (Dan. 9:27). (15) He introduces an idolatrous worship (Dan. 9:27) in which he sets himself up as god (Dan. 11:36-37; 2 Thess. 2:4; Rev.

13:5). (16) He bears the characterization of a blasphemer because of the assumption of deity (Ezek. 28:2; Dan. 7:25; Rev. 13:1, 5-6). (17) This one is energized by Satan (Ezek. 28:9-12; Rev. 13:4), receives his authority from him, and is controlled by the pride of the devil (Ezek. 28:2; Dan. 8:25). (18) He is the head of Satan's lawless system (2 Thess. 2:4) and his claim to power and to deity is proved by signs wrought through satanic power (2 Thess. 2:9-10). (19) He is received as God and as ruler because of the blindness of the people (2 Thess. 2:11). (20) This ruler becomes the great adversary of Israel (Dan. 7:21, 25; 8:24; Rev. 13:7). (21) There will come an alliance against him (Ezek. 28:7; Dan. 11:40-41) which will contest his authority. (22) In the ensuing conflict he will gain control over Palestine and adjacent territory (Dan. 11:42) and will make his headquarters in Jerusalem (Dan. 11:45). (23) This ruler, at the time of his rise to power, is elevated through the instrumentality of the harlot, the corrupt religious system, which consequently seeks to dominate him (Rev. 17:3). (24) This system is destroyed by the ruler so that he may rule unhindered (Rev. 17:16-17). (25) He becomes the special adversary of the Prince of Princes (Dan. 8:25), His program (2 Thess. 2:4; Rev. 17:14), and His people (Dan. 7:21, 25; 8:24; Rev. 13:7). (26) While he continues in power for seven years (Dan. 9:27), his satanic activity is confined to the last half of the tribulation period (Dan. 7:25; 9:27; 11:36; Rev. 13:5). (27) His rule will be terminated by a direct judgment from God (Ezek. 28:6; Dan. 7:22, 26; 8:25; 9:27; 11:45; Rev. 19:19-20). This judgment will take place as he is engaged in a military campaign in Palestine (Ezek. 28:8-9; Rev. 19:19), and he will be cast into the lake of fire (Rev. 19:20; Ezek. 28:10). (28) This judgment will take place at the second advent of Christ (2 Thess. 2:8; Dan. 7:22) and will constitute a manifestation of His Messianic authority (Rev. 11:15). (29) The kingdom over which he ruled will pass to the authority of the Messiah and will become the kingdom of the saints (Dan. 7:27).[1]

INVASION

One of the most terrifying events of the last week of years is the breaking out of conflict between the world power coalitions. The battleground is Palestine; the chief sufferers the Jews.

The battle that marks the outbreak of the world war is described most completely in Ezekiel 38—39.

Ezekiel 38:1-6. The participants in the invasion are identified as Russia and its confederates, coming from the "remote parts of the north" (v. 6) with many peoples.

Ezekiel 38:7-9. Israel's people, having returned from "many nations" (v. 8), are finally dwelling securely (possibly because of a foretold treaty with the Western power).

Ezekiel 38:10-14. In spite of a Western protest (v. 13), the invaders sweep down on defenseless Israel to plunder her.

Ezekiel 38:14-16. The invading army is successful, covering the land like a cloud, for (like earlier invaders) they are called to this ministry of judgment by God, that Israel might be purged and the invader's sin punished.

Ezekiel 38:17-23. In a great cataclysm of nature,

God then acts to destroy the invading army. The destruction is so startling and so focused on Russia and her allies that its supernatural origins are recognized. "And I shall magnify Myself, sanctify Myself, and make Myself known in the sight of many nations; and they will know that I am the Lord" (v. 23).

Ezekiel 39:9-11. The remaining war materiel becomes a natural resource for the Jewish rebuilding of the land. Months pass before the dead can be disposed of (vv. 11-16). This battle is followed (again, remember that the time sequences and gaps are not specifically defined in prophecy) by the cleansing of Israel, their forgiveness and restoration, and the vindication of God's holiness in the sight of the entire earth (vv. 21-29).

Some of the questions most often raised about this battle are: When does it take place? Is this Armageddon, the final battle?

While many different suggestions have been raised, it is probably best to see this as an event in the middle of Daniel's seventh week, an event that, with the destruction of the Russian powers, creates a power vacuum into which the Antichrist and the West quickly move.

Several things seem to indicate this as the best interpretation. Israel is in her land. The world seems to be experiencing security rather than the terrible judgments of the culminating tribulations. The Antichrist has not yet established world power; the other power blocs prevent this. But with the threat of Russia removed, there is nothing to hinder

CONTRASTS

Gog/Magog Invasion	Armageddon
Gog and allies involved (Joel 3:2; Zeph. 3:8; Zech. 12:3; 14:2)	All nations involved
Invasion from north (Ezek. 38:6, 15; 39:2)	Gather from whole earth
Gog invades for a spoil (Ezek. 38:11-12)	Nations gather to destroy God's people
Gog is head of the armies (Ezek. 38:7; Rev. 19:19)	The Beast (Antichrist) heads the armies
Gog overthrown by cataclysm (Ezek. 38:22; Rev. 19:15)	Armies destroyed by the sword from Christ's mouth (the Word)

the ultimate grasping of power. The West is free to occupy Palestine and the adjacent oil fields of the OPEC nations. In Jerusalem, the Antichrist is free to demand worship and set up an image of himself in the restored Temple. With this ultimate uncovering of evil, the culminating judgments on earth begin.

ARMAGEDDON

The final battle also is prophesied to take place in Palestine. But this battle, called Armageddon (for its location near the hill of Megiddo, about ten miles south of Nazareth and fifteen miles inland from the Mediterranean), concludes with the personal appearance of the Messiah and His personal destruction of the armies involved, so that the promised

Messianic Kingdom of peace and righteousness can be set up. While again being aware of time traps, it does seem that with the disposal of the Antichrist and his associated leaders all opposition to the Messiah has been removed; the Kingdom is ready for its King.

These and other contrasts suggest that the great final Battle of Armageddon is not the battle described by Ezekiel but that once again we are being given insight into some of the many, complex, climactic events of history.

And once again, looking at the political situation of our own day, we see the ease with which the events foretold could come to pass with sudden and unexpected swiftness! Destiny is approaching.

In spite of the hint of springtime in the air, the shape of destiny seems dark indeed.

GOING DEEPER

to personalize

1. Read carefully Ezekiel 38 and 39. Then read Joel 2. How do these two passages seem to be related?

2. It is clear from the Pentecost quote on pages 145-48 that students of prophecy do relate the Old and New Testament revelations. For a taste of New Testament prophecy, read carefully Revelation 13 and Revelation 17. To what Old Testament prophecies can you relate the pictures drawn here? Do some elements seem *not* to reflect Old Testament prophecy?

3. Add to your chart on the seventieth week (page 111) any new material that seems to fit. Are you beginning to get a picture of the events of the seventieth week and their relationship?

How does your picture of events agree with or disagree with this summary of Pentecost's view?

(1) Israel makes a false covenant with the beast (Anti-Christ) and occupies her land in a false security (Dan. 9:27; Ezek. 38:8, 11)
(2) Russia invades Palestine (Ezek. 38:11; Joel 2:1-21)
(3) The Beast breaks his covenant with Israel and occupies the land (Dan. 11:41-45)
(4) Russia and allies are destroyed (Ezek. 39:1-4)
(5) A world government under the Beast is formed (Rev. 13)
(6) All nations gather to battle around Jerusalem (Zech. 14:1-3)
(7) Messiah/Jesus returns to destroy all Gentile world powers and take up rule himself (Zech. 12:1-9; Isa. 33:1-24; Rev. 20:7-10)

to probe

1. On a world map, draw the boundaries of the four great world power blocs identified in Bible prophecy as the end time begins.

2. One of the most puzzling questions concerning prophecy is: How does the United States fit in? What do prophecy writers think? How do they deal with the question? Do some research, and write up your own view in a report.

1. J. Dwight Pentecost, *Things to Come* (Grand Rapids: Zondervan, 1958), pp. 333-34.
2. Ibid.

12

selected prophets

THE GLORIOUS KINGDOM

READING ABOUT THE EVENTS sketched in the last two chapters, it's all too easy to feel steam-rollered. The end of history is marked by great sweeping events; individuals are caught up in movements beyond their control; world leaders, with the most evil and selfish of motives, manipulate events to their own supposed advantage.

And behind it all is God.

Permitting. Using the plots of His enemies for His own ends.

In this dramatic prophetic portrait of the grinding clash of massive forces, the individual is lost from view. Helpless in a world gone mad, the individual seems not only powerless but unimportant. All the elements in our own culture that tend to depersonalize are magnified a thousand times, and in the great upheaval that marks the culmination of history, individual freedom and dignity seem to be gone indeed.

But this is deceptive. The events deal with the masses—but even in this maelstrom, God's eye remains on each individual. The ultimate reality behind the universe and behind history itself is personal, not impersonal. And the goal always in God's mind is good.

He is concerned for righteousness, that true goodness might be restored.

He is concerned for relationship, that in Him individuals and mankind might find the fulfillment for which each of us strains.

THE PROMISED RULER

The personal nature of Old Testament prophecy is nowhere seen as clearly as in the teaching that the time of promised blessing will be introduced by God's Man.

This theme was introduced in the Davidic Covenant, and was often repeated by the prophets.

In the earliest days, the promised throne was said to be the Lord's own (1 Chron. 28: 5; 2 Chron. 9: 8; 13: 8). The King is "God with us" (Isa. 7: 14), to be born of a virgin in Bethlehem (Isa. 11: 1-5; Jer. 23: 5; Ezek. 34: 23; 37: 24; Hos. 3: 4-5; Mic. 5: 2). The extent of this ruler's authority is the entire world (Psa. 2: 8; Isa. 11: 9; 42: 4; Jer. 23: 5; Zech. 14: 9), even though it will be centered in Jerusalem (Isa. 2: 1-3; 62: 1-7; Zech. 8: 20-23). Ruling over a converted Israel (Isa. 11: 11-12; 14: 1-2; Jer. 23: 6-8; 32: 37-38; 33: 7-9; Ezek. 37: 21-25; Mic. 4: 6-8), the kingdom will extend to bring peace to Gentiles as

TITLES OF THE COMING KING

Lord of Hosts (Isa. 24:23)
The Lord (Mic. 4:7)
Thy God (Isa. 52:7)
The most High (Dan. 7:22-24)
The Lord our Righteousness (Jer. 23:6)
Son of God (Isa. 9:6)
Ancient of Days (Dan. 7:13)
Jehovah (Isa. 2:2-4)
The King (Isa. 33:17)
Messiah the Prince (Dan. 9:25-26)
The Judge (Isa. 11:3-4)
The Redeemer (Isa. 59:20)
The Lawgiver (Isa. 33:22)
Prince of Princes (Dan. 8:25)

well (Psa. 72:11, 17; 86:9; Isa. 55:5; Dan. 7:13-14; Mic. 4:2; Zech. 8:22).

All of the blessings promised under the original Abrahamic Covenant and the later New Covenant are seen to be dependent on the presence of the King, who can make them real. That the King must be God Himself, incarnated as a man, was recognized by the prophets, even if misunderstood later by the generation that rejected Jesus of Nazareth. Isaiah wrote,

> A child will be born to us, a son will be given to us;
> And the government will rest on His shoulders.
> And His name will be called Wonderful Counselor, Mighty God,
> Eternal Father, Prince of Peace.

There will be no end to the increase of His government or of peace,
On the throne of David and over his kingdom,
To establish it and to uphold it with justice and righteousness
From then on and forevermore.

Isaiah 9:6-7

His titles alone make His deity and authority totally clear.

The thrust of these and many other teachings of the Old Testament is that the time of the end is in fact *the* time for God's final personal intervention in our cosmos. In the presence of the great King of Kings Himself, the deeply personal nature of His continuing concern and love for His creatures will be shown.

Warped. The terror of the end times, to be seen in true perspective, must be held up against the backdrop of human sin. Ever since Adam, men have turned and twisted away from God, seeking to find some way to live other than in relationship with Him. The recorded history of men and nations, with its countless repeated and brutal conflicts, the pride and hatred and anger and selfishness that have taken even the good gifts of God and twisted them, make it abundantly clear that man must be rescued from himself. Time and time again God in the past has given men new starts. Yet soon sin has reasserted itself, and the new has become as grim and painful as the old.

Finally, with all divine restraint released, the great

rebellion of the end time will show just how sinful sin is. With every mask stripped away, the inhumanity of a humankind cast adrift will be fully known. The time of the end is not God's doing; it is His permission for sin's ultimate unveiling . . . and the goal is that, in the unveiling, God might act to stamp out the disease that has sickened us all.

The terror comes when we see that unleashed sin is unresponsive to God. Even when He is fully revealed in the majesty of His judgment, there is no repentance.

Restored. People often speak of what "might have been." For us, "might have been's" can never be recaptured. But after Messiah subdues the rebels and punishes those who will not respond to His love, the world finally will come to know what might have been.

"If only Adam had not eaten the fruit! What a wonderful garden of Eden the world might have become." If you've had such thoughts, you know at least the direction of human experience after the Messiah sets up His rule. Then, finally, what might have been will become real. The goodness and love of God's original design for man will be realized by all.

In looking at the picture of the world under Messiah's rule and the joys experienced by His people, we come to know in a uniquely different way how tragic that first rebellion was. The final anguished upheaval of the tribulation is in fact the most personal of divine interventions, by which God reaches out to stop the downward rush, to bring a restored people to personal relationship again.

In the person of the Messiah King, God Himself acts in history's final judgment and sets things right.

DESCRIPTIONS OF HIS RULE

What will this might-have-been restoration be like? The Old Testament is full of descriptions of the Messianic age. Isaiah's is among the most famous:

> Then a shoot will spring from the stem of Jesse,
> And a branch from his roots will be a fruit.
> And the Spirit of the Lord will rest on Him,
> The Spirit of wisdom and understanding,
> The spirit of counsel and strength,
> The spirit of knowledge and the fear of the Lord.
> And He will delight in the fear of the Lord.
> And He will not judge by what His eyes see,
> Nor make a decision by what His ears hear;
> But with righteousness He will judge the poor,
> And decide with fairness for the afflicted of the earth;
> And He will strike the earth with the rod of His mouth,
> And with the breath of His lips He will slay the wicked.
> Also righteousness will be the belt about His loins,
> And faithfulness the belt about his waist.
> And the wolf will dwell with the lamb,
> And the leopard will lie down with the kid,
> And the calf and the young lion and the fatling together;

And a little boy will lead them.
Also the cow and the bear will graze;
Their young will lie down together;
And the lion will eat straw like the ox.
And the nursing child will play by the hole of the cobra,
And the weaned child will put his hand on the viper's den.
They will not hurt or destroy in all My holy mountain,
For the earth will be full of the knowledge of the Lord
As the waters cover the sea.

Isaiah 11:1-9

In this extended passage we see a number of themes often repeated elsewhere. The supernaturally endowed ruler brings peace. The poor and oppressed are finally cared for. The wicked are judged, as righteousness and faithfulness are affirmed as the values by which men live. Great changes take place in the physical universe, with the very nature of the carnivorous animals affected.

While the physical changes are perhaps as drastic as those portrayed in early Genesis prior to the flood (see Gen. 2:4-6), of greater importance is the impact of the Messiah's rule on the condition of man.

- In place of *war* there will be *peace* (Isa. 9:4-7; 32:17-18; Ezek. 34:25, 28; Mic. 4:2-3).
- In place of *sin* there will be *holiness* (Isa. 29:18-23; 35:8-9; Zeph. 3:11, 13; Zech. 14:20-21).
- In place of *misery* there will be *comfort* (Isa.

29:22-23; 61:3-7; 66:13; Jer. 31:23-25; Zech. 9:11-12).

- In place of *injustice* there will be *justice* (Isa. 42:1-4; 65:21-23; Jer. 31:23; 29:30).
- In place of *sickness* there will be *healing* (Isa. 29:17-19), 35:3-6; 61:1-2; Jer. 31:8; Mic. 4:6-7).
- In place of *ignorance* will be the *knowledge of God* (Isa. 11:1-2, 9; 41:19-20; 54:13; Hab. 2:14).
- Instead of *early death* will come *preservation* (Isa. 41:8-14; 62:8-9; Jer. 23:6; 32:27; Ezek. 34:27; Joel 3:16-17; Zech. 8:14-15; 9:17; 14:10-11).
- Instead of *poverty* there will be *prosperity* (Isa. 4:1; 30:12-15; 65:21-22; Ezek. 34:26; Joel 2:21-27; Amos 9:13-14; Zech. 8:11-22; 9:16-17).

All these and many other blessings to mankind are promised by the Old Testament prophets . . . when the King finally comes.

THE END?

Is this then to be the end? A Kingdom established here on earth, ruled over by the Messiah, populated by a converted multitiude?

Certainly it would seem so from the Old Testament perspective. Everything that characterizes the Messianic Kingdom is to be the endless possession of the redeemed race. Joel proclaims, "Judah will be inhabited forever, and Jerusalem to all generations" (3:20). Isaiah says, "My salvation shall be forever, and My righteousness shall not wane" (51:6). For Isaiah, the prospect of the foretold future is a bright star, calling God's people everywhere on to hope:

Violence will not be heard again in your land,
Nor devastation or destruction within your borders;
But you will call your walls salvation, and your gates praise.
No longer will you have the sun for light by day,
Nor for brightness will the moon give you light;
But you will have the Lord for an everlasting light,
And your God for your glory.
Your sun will set no more
Neither will your moon wane;
For you will have the Lord for an everlasting light,
And the days of your mourning will be finished.
Then all your people will be righteous;
They will possess the land for ever.

Isaiah 60:18-21

Picking up this theme in a prophetic vision given to him on Patmos, the New Testament writer John looks beyond the earthly Kingdom and writes,

> Then I saw a new heaven and a new earth, for the first heaven and the first earth had passed away, and there was no longer any sea. I saw the Holy City, the new Jerusalem, coming down out of heaven from God, prepared as a bride beautifully dressed for her husband. And I heard a loud voice from the throne saying, "Now the dwelling of God is with men, and he will live with them. They will be his people, and God himself will be with them and be their God. He will wipe every tear from their eyes. There will be no more death or mourn-

ing or crying or pain, for the old order of things has passed away.

Revelation 21:1-4

Certainly the prophetic picture given in Old and New Testament is complex. But knowing how accurately prophecies have been fulfilled, we can hardly doubt that somehow the complex picture harmonizes into one glorious whole. When destiny arrives, and we discover *our* place, then we too will know the full meaning of that springtime the ancients glimpsed and yearned for.

GOING DEEPER

to personalize

1. On the next page is a listing of the prophets' pictures of the coming Kingdom. Look up ten references and then react to your findings guided by *personalize* 3 below. (Or, skip this item, and do *personalize* 2.)

2. Examine the Bible references listed on pages 159-60 dealing with the impact of Messiah's rule on the condition of human life. Then react to your findings guided by number 3 below.

3. If you lived in Old Testament times, which of the aspects of the future Kingdom would seem most important to you? List *five* "important to me" things about the Kingdom. Then *rank* them from most important to least important. Finally, write briefly on each item, explaining its significance to you.

4. From the perspective of a person living today, which aspect of the coming Kingdom seems most

The prophets' Kingdom view

Isaiah	2:1-4	Ezekiel	20:33-42
	4:2-6		34:20-31
	9:6-7		36:22-36
	11:1-13		37:1-28
	24:1-23		39:21-29
	32:1-5, 14-20	Hosea	3:4-5
	33:17-24	Joel	2:28—3:2
	35:1-10		3:9-21
	52:7-10	Amos	9:9-15
	60:1—61:6	Obadiah	15-21
	66:15-23	Micah	4:1-5
Jeremiah	22:1-8	Zephaniah	3:8-20
	31:1-27	Haggai	2:1-9
	33:14-26	Zechariah	2:1-13
Daniel	2:31-45		6:11-13
	7:1-28		8:1-8, 20-23
	9:1-3, 20-27		9:9-10
	12:1-4		12:1-10
Malachi	3:1-5		14:1-21
	4:1-6		

important to you? List three most important aspects for a believer today. How do these differ from the items listed under 3 above (if they do)? How do you explain the difference?

5. Finally, read 1 Corinthians 15:24-28. What implications does this hold for the "endless" nature of the Messianic Kingdom?

to probe

1. In this chapter we've looked at a Messianic

earthly Kingdom associated with Messiah's rule as King. Is this the only kingdom mentioned in Scripture? Use a concordance and see if additional aspects of God's Kingdom are revealed.

2. Continue to work on your chart of the seventieth week. What would you add or change at this point?

3. The Messianic Kingdom of the Old Testament is often called the "millennial kingdom"or "millennium," from a reference in Revelation 20: 1-6. Study this passage, and see what it seems to add to the Old Testament picture. Or does it not fit the Old Testament picture? Write out your own position—*then* find two books on prophecy or two commentaries and see how the authors understand this passage.

13

selected New Testament passages

OLD TESTAMENT . . . OR NEW?

WHEN I WAS A BOY in Michigan, I used to stoke the furnace for the old minister from our small-town church. Each morning on the way to school I'd stop off, go down to the basement, dig the chunks of slag from the banked coals, and add more fuel. Then when a bucket of slag had been collected, I'd bring it up the stairs for him, and leave it outside on the icy doorstep.

I don't remember much about him, except that he was a fine-looking man, tall, white-haired, with a lined face. And I do remember one thing he used to say to me: that someday I'd die and become an angel.

I didn't know then whether he was wrong or right, but I wasn't at all sure I wanted the promised wings. Somehow the prospect of lounging on a cloud and plucking a harp didn't seem like an adequate destiny for an active boy. Of course, if God wanted it that way, it would be all right. But . . .

ADEQUATE DESTINY?

Just as the Old Testament believer tended to simplify the future and see only the glories of the Messianic Kingdom, so Christians tend to oversimplify. We have a much more clearly defined picture of the future given in the New Testament—at least more clear in that several unexpected dimensions of God's plan have now been explained.

The New Testament, for instance, speaks much more clearly of resurrection. It tends to emphasize more both the eternal punishment of the rebel and the eternal blessedness of the individual who has come to a personal relationship with God through Jesus. While the Old Testament emphasizes the Messianic Kingdom to be established on earth, the New Testament stresses an eternal state when, after a final rebellion, this earth and the universe are dissolved with a fiery heat (2 Peter 3:8-18) and, following final judgment, a new heavens and earth are created for God and man.

The New Testament also speaks about what happens to the individual believer when he dies, awaiting that great resurrection. Rather than returning to the earth, as do the animals, the human personality is translated to the presence of God and given an intermediate body (2 Cor. 5:1-5). To "die and go to heaven" really is *not* the end, not for the individual nor for God's plan.

While the New Testament does not confront us on every page with a reminder of the complexity of God's springtime, it unquestionably reveals much about the future. To understand it, we must see it in relationship to what is contained in the Old.

It is also clear that some themes from the New Testament add to our understanding of the Old, because they were really not part of that revelation. In fact, the whole intervening age between the sixty-ninth and seventieth weeks is said to be a "mystery" (Eph. 3:9), something previously hidden but now revealed by God. In speaking about that age, Jesus referred to this Old Testament passage:

> I will open my mouth in parables;
> I will utter things hidden since the creation of the world.
>
> *Matthew 13:35 quoting Psalm 78:2*

Colossians speaks of the Church as a body of believers linked to Jesus the Head, a living organism, not merely an organization or community. It calls this a "mystery that has been kept hidden for ages and generations, but is now disclosed to the saints" (1:26). Thus the Church is portrayed not as some mystical fulfillment of the promises to Israel but as a new dimension of God's plan, hidden from the prophets and saints of Old Testament times.

In fact, it is fair to say that *everything that happens between the ending of Daniel's sixty-ninth week and the beginning of the seventieth* (with the exception of the death of the Messiah and the destruction of Jerusalem) *is not the subject of Old Testament prophecy.* It is probable that many new dimensions of the future revealed in the New Testament (such as the

Rapture in 1 Thessalonians 4:13-18) are not located in the time periods covered in Old Testament prophecy at all! If this is correct, the coming of Christ for believers of this age—His Church—*would* take place before the tribulation. And the final rebellion would take place at the end of the Messianic Kingdom period and be the last expression of evil permitted in the universe, ushering in the final judgment.

MAJOR NEW TESTAMENT PASSAGES

There are several major New Testament passages that are closely coordinated with Old Testament prophecy. While these will be discussed at length in the New Testament books of the **Bible Alive Series,** it's important now to notice that the repetition of themes from Old Testament revelation makes it clear that God has *not* set aside His promises or His announced intentions.

Matthew 24:3–25:46. Here Christ answers His disciples' questions about the end of the age and the sign of His coming. He suggests a sudden increase of wars, famines, and earthquakes as the first indication. Soon there will be an intensified persecution of the Jewish people. The " 'abomination that causes desolation,' spoken of through the prophet Daniel" (24:15) will be the first conclusive sign that these troubles are part of the tribulation period.

Following the tribulation of those days comes Jesus' own appearance as a conqueror, "coming on the clouds of the sky, with power and great glory"

(24:30), to gather the chosen ones from throughout the earth.

Christ makes it very clear that this coming of His will be unexpected by mankind in general (24:36-41). Believers are to watch expectantly and be prepared for the return. Much of chapter 25 is given to exhorting watchfulness. Here Christ points out that those who have destiny in view will be motivated to serve Him rather than be drawn off into empty activities—that each servant of His will be judged for how he behaved while the Master was absent (25:14-30).

The passage closes with a picture of judgment on the Gentile world, identified there as "the nations" (25:32). The basis of their evaluation will be their treatment of the King's Jewish brothers and sisters during the terrible days when everyone seems bent on persecuting them (25:31-40). As a result, the enemy will be sent to immediate judgment while the blessed will be welcomed to life in "the kingdom prepared for you since the creation of the world" (v. 34).

Undoubtedly this picture of the future drawn by Christ recapitulates the vision of the prophets. Christ Himself expects the Old Testament word about the future to stand.

Romans 9–11. In this extended portion Paul answers those who object to Christianity because it seemed to set aside God's Old Testament people. Their charge is that either God is not faithful to His promises, and so cannot be trusted—or that the faith proclaimed by Paul is false.

The great apostle answers the critics in ways that reaffirm both the distinctiveness of the New Covenant community and the trustworthiness of the Old Testament portrait of destiny.

Paul argues that while the Jews have many advantages, simply being a Jew is no guarantee of God's favor. God in history has always acted to *choose* out individuals as recipients of His blessing. Also, the Old Testament did foretell a time when Gentiles would come to know God. Certainly, then, a Church in which Jew and Gentile meet as common recipients of the grace of God is not in violation of the Old Testament Covenants (Rom. 9).

In fact, Israel's unresponsiveness to God has always been at the root of every past experience of being temporarily set aside. The present blessing and welcome of the Gentiles in Christ is to make Israel jealous, and call her back to God.

But Israel is unresponsive still! What then will God do? "Did God reject his people?" Paul asks. And he answers, "By no means! . . . God has not rejected his people, whom he foreknew" (11:1-2). God's continuing commitment is seen first in the many individual Jews who accept Jesus as Savior. Thus a remnant is being preserved now, as in past history. But even more: Israel, like the broken-off branch of a tree, will be grafted back in. The promised national conversion will come. Paul promises:

> And so all Israel will be saved, as it is written:
> "The Deliverer will come from Zion;
> he will turn godlessness away from Jacob.

And this is My covenant with them
when I take away their sins."

Romans 11:26-27

The great apostle, the man through whom God chose to give us the majority of our New Testament's teaching, firmly believed that God's Old Testament promises hold firm and the future springtime of the prophets *will* come.

1 Corinthians 15. In this chapter Paul is dealing with resurrection, a theme mentioned in the Old Testament but developed much more completely in the New in the wake of Jesus' resurrection. In this connection, Paul envisions an end *beyond* the Messianic Kingdom of the prophets.

> Then the end will come, when he [Christ] hands over the kingdom to God the Father after he has destroyed all dominion, authority and power. For he must reign until God has put all his enemies under his feet. The last enemy to be destroyed is death. For God "has put everything under his feet" [Ps. 8:6]. Now when it says that "everything" has been put under him, it is clear that this does not include God himself, who put everything under Christ. When he has done this, then the Son himself will be made subject to him who put everything under him, so that God may be all in all.
>
> *1 Corinthians 15:24-28*

2 Thessalonians. In this New Testament letter

Paul's purpose is to clarify misunderstood teaching about the future, given while he was in Thessalonica. Paul apparently just touches on aspects about which the believers there had become confused.

He speaks of Jesus' return to earth in judgment and vengeance (1:7-10). He makes it clear that this return will not pass unnoticed; in fact, it cannot come until the Antichrist is revealed and enters the Temple, proclaiming himself to be God—a clear reference to Daniel's seventieth week (2:1-8). Paul goes on to describe the satanic power given the Antichrist and the influence he exerts over the ungodly (2:9-12).

In his final chapter, Paul exhorts holy living in view of the Lord's coming. Surely this world has nothing that those who look beyond time and see the approach of destiny could desire.

Revelation. We'll look into the book of Revelation in the last book of the **Bible Alive Series,** *His Glory.* For now, it is enough to note that, while we see new dimensions of the tribulation period unfolded and for the first time learn the length of the Messianic Kingdom, the primary source for understanding Revelation's prophecies is again the Old Testament picture of the future. If we take the Old Testament picture seriously, we have a basis for understanding seemingly obscure references in the final book of our New Testament.

What is important for us to see is simply this: the New Testament revelation does not *supercede* or *replace* the Old. It builds on the foundation laid by prophets and apostles. It often adds to our understanding of events foretold in the Old; it sometimes adds totally unexpected aspects and dimensions to past revelation. But Old and New Testaments are revelations of one and the same God. They do not contradict each other; they complement.

In both Testaments, we are given an invitation to watch for springtime. And warned to be ready!

WHY PROPHECY?

This is a last question we need to consider. What is the value of prophecy for us today? We can't control or change the future. Why should we be told so much about it? Especially when we are exhorted to live for the Lord *today*.

I am sure that we are not given prophetic portraits of the destiny that awaits us so we can play games with the Scripture, construct our own sequence and time schemes, and argue about the likelihood of pre-, mid-, or posttribulation Raptures. Instead, the Bible's revelation of springtime is meant to have a definite impact on our faith and our commitment to God.

We see this clearly in Peter, who describes the destruction by fire of "the present heavens and earth" (2 Pet. 3:7) and then adds:

> Since everything will be destroyed in this way, what kind of people ought you to be? You ought to live holy and godly lives as you look forward to the day of God and speed its coming.
>
> *2 Peter 3:11-12*

The writer to the Hebrews reflects this same awareness of our world's impermanence and the emptiness of the dreams that capture the human heart.

> Now he has promised, "Once more I will shake not only the earth but also the heavens." The words "once more" indicate the removing of what can be shaken—that is, created things—so that what cannot be shaken may remain.
>
> Therefore, since we are receiving a kingdom that cannot be shaken, let us be thankful, and so worship God acceptably with reverence and awe, for our God is a consuming fire.
>
> *Hebrews 12:26-29*

How easily the values and valuables of this world draw our attention away from God. How quickly we become entranced with the tinsel of a universe that one day soon will be shaken and removed. How much more worthwhile to turn our attention to offering God not only due reverence and awe but our loyalty and lives as well.

This is the real value of prophecy for believers in any age. When this world and its attractions dominate our thoughts and hopes, we are called by God to look ahead to springtime. Straining forward, we are invited to reach out toward destiny and to see in the march of our own history the form of One swiftly approaching.

There He is!

Just over the horizon of our time . . . in the person of Jesus the Messiah, our destiny lies in that great eternity ahead.

GOING DEEPER

to personalize

1. Jot down what you recall of your impressions of the future before we began this springtime study. How have they changed?

2. How have *you* changed? Has this study of prophecy had any impact on your values, attitudes, or life-style? Try to be specific in describing what impact.

3. Look over either Matthew 24—25 or Romans 9—11 and jot down your ideas about the kind of impact its teaching might well have on a Christian today.

4. The author mentions one value of studying prophecy on pages 173-74. Can you think of other values? (For instance, see 1 Thessalonians 4:13-18. See if you can locate any additional passages with suggested values expressed.)

5. Paul concludes Romans 11 with a great doxology, caught up by his amazement at the complexity of God's great plan for mankind and its multifaceted culmination. Why not read and meditate on that passage as we conclude our study of *Springtime Coming*? You'll find it in Romans 11:33-36.

to probe

1. Many, many aspects of prophecy have not been touched in this survey, and many questions have not been explored. One of these is the identification of Israel and the Church. Are these peoples of God the same or different? Or, how are they similar and how

do they differ? When we read an Old Testament promise to Israel, can we take it for ourselves as well? Study this question and, as a final project, *without referring to any commentary or outside aid,* write a carefully reasoned explanation of your ideas.

2. Develop an interview form containing ten questions about the future, and interview at least ten churchgoers. Your questions should be designed to find out something about the respondent's knowledge of the coming destiny and also to find out something about his application of that knowledge. That is, does his grasp of the future affect his life, and if so, how?

3. Outline (and if possible, preach) a prophetic sermon. Be sure to define carefully your aim, which should be expressed in a *purpose sentence.* Then develop your message to achieve this purpose.

Period	Theme	Books
I. PRIMEVAL PERIOD	CREATION Creation to Abraham	*Genesis 1–11* *Job*
II. PATRIARCHAL PERIOD (2166-1446)*	COVENANT Abraham to Moses	*Genesis 12–50*
III. EXODUS PERIOD (1446-1406)	LAW Moses' Leadership	*Exodus* *Numbers* *Leviticus* *Deuteronomy*
IV. CONQUEST OF CANAAN (1406-1390)	CONQUEST Joshua's Leadership	*Joshua*
V. TIME OF JUDGES (1367-1050)	JUDGES No Leadership	*Judges* *Ruth* *I Samuel 1–7*
VI. UNITED KINGDOM (1050-931)	KINGDOM Monarchy Established	*I Samuel 8–11* *II Samuel 1–24* *I Kings 1–11* *I Chronicles* *II Chronicles*
	Establishment (David)	*Psalms*
	Decline (Solomon)	*Ecclesiastes* *Proverbs* *Song of Solomon*

*The dates are taken from *A Survey of Israel's History* by Leon Wood (Grand Rapids: Zondervan, 1975).

VII. DIVIDED KINGDOM (931-722) Israel Elijah Elisha Judah	PROPHETIC MOVEMENT Two Kingdoms	*I Kings 12–22* *II Kings 1–17* *II Chronicles 10–29* *Jonah* *Obadiah* *Amos* *Hosea* *Micah* *Joel* *Isaiah*
VIII. SURVIVING KINGDOM (722-586)	Judah Remains	*II Kings 18–25* *II Chronicles 30–36* *Jeremiah* *Nahum* *Zephaniah* *Habakkuk*
IX. BABYLONIAN CAPTIVITY **(586-538)**	**JUDGMENT** **Torn from Palestine**	***Ezekiel*** ***Daniel*** ***Esther***
X. RESTORATION **(538-400)**	**The Jews Return** *400 Years Between the Testaments*	***Ezra*** ***Nehemiah*** ***Haggai*** ***Zechariah*** ***Malachi***

Leader Supplement

SPRINGTIME COMING

THE NATURE OF BIBLE SURVEY

THIS BOOK IS PART of a series that surveys both the Old and New Testaments. As a survey book, it differs significantly from other approaches to examining the Bible.

Introduction books tend to focus on details about the Bible. They examine historical and cultural backgrounds, discuss arguments for canonicity, struggle with dating, and argue for or against such things as two Daniels, the identity of the Twelve, and other scholarly questions. Issues dealt with in introduction are important, but survey is not primarily concerned with them.

Apologetics books are primarily concerned with the defense of some view of Scripture or with resolving some historical or philosophical problem. Like books of introduction, apologetics approaches tend to talk *about* the Bible, comparing Bible miracle stories, for instance, with similar stories in non-Christian and later Christian traditions, etc. Apologetics has a place. But survey is not concerned primarily with the defense of Scripture or of faith.

Commentaries, which *are* concerned with the text, tend to go into close detail on words and phrases. In their intensive examination they often explore questions of introduction and apologetics as well. Commentaries are helpful for detailed study of a single book of Scripture or as references in which to check questions about verses or phrases we don't understand. But again, a survey approach does not attempt to do the job of a commentary.

Sermon thoughts are often the subject of books about the text of Scripture. These tend to focus on application or inspiration and, again, these have value. But they are not survey. Survey focuses attention on mastery of both the *content* of Scripture and its *message.*

In the most significant sense, Bible survey brings us to a study of Bible content. In survey we are not so much concerned about what people may say about the Bible; we are concerned with what the Bible says. It is the text itself, what God is saying to us, that we are eager to master. His message to us in the Word is the orienting thrust of survey study.

This concern helps determine our approach to our study. We want to motivate our students to *discover what the Scripture is saying–and to apply its message to their lives.* The textbook and classroom process are designed to achieve these twin goals. The textbooks orient the reader to the passages to be explored; questions at the end of each chapter lead him or her into the Bible for personal study of the Word. These are designed to help the student explore both the content and the message—both meaning and application.

The classroom process, outlined in this supplement, suggests a variety of methods you can use to draw out your students, to help them share what they have learned, to help them share with one another and motivate one another to respond to God's Word. In this classroom process, you are not so much an expert or a lecturer as you are a *facilitator*–someone who helps the learners think through the meaning of what they have studied before class and apply that truth to their own lives. Working with the Teacher, the Holy Spirit, your goal is to help your students open their lives to Him and to His Word.

In this process, your students will develop a mastery of the content of Scripture—a vital overview of the Word. They will learn methods of personal Bible study. They will discover how to listen for the message God is communicating to each of us through His Word. In survey, the Bible—so often a closed book even to believers—begins to make sense and to come alive.

What are the specific advantages of a survey approach, which focuses attention on the content of Scripture and its message rather than on speculation *about* Scripture?

1. *You give students a foundation for a lifetime of Bible study.* Initial acquaintance with the whole Bible, an acquaintance that motivates and opens up the Bible for later in-depth study, is a basic contribution of survey.

2. *You give students an orientation to Scripture's sweep and theme.* Most Christians today are ignorant of these. They do not know the Bible's major themes and emphases; they do not know how revelation was given by God across the centuries and decades. Survey makes a unique contribution by "putting it all together" for the reader, sensitizing us in a distinct way to the place of each book in the Bible and its message for us.

3. *You give students vital tools for study.* A person who understands how the Bible fits together is able to interpret it more accurately than one who grasps at a verse and applies it without knowing the setting or purpose of God when that word was first spoken. Survey gives a vital study tool in teaching the learner to see the Word first in terms of the men and women of the day when it was spoken, and showing how application flows out of this initial interpretation.

Each of these benefits can be ours when we come to Scripture to master its contents and listen to its message. And each will be—as we work together through these Old Testament prophets in this portion of our **Bible Alive** survey.

In these survey studies, you will give your students insight into Old Testament prophecy and discover the striking portrait of future history developed in the Scriptures. You will provide a mastery of the post-exilic books of the Old Testament as well as give your students a distinctive grasp of major prophetic themes. You will help them apply the message of each theme to their own lives now. In all this you'll see God use His Word in your students' lives. Scripture does speak to us today. In the Bible survey studies you and your students will hear God's voice and be drawn into closer relationship with Him.

APPROACHES TO SURVEY

BIBLE SURVEY CAN BE approached in several ways. One is thematic: taking a topic like "law" and tracing it through the Old Testament, then moving on to another topic to do the same. A second approach is to focus on groupings of books, such as the Pentateuch or the poetical books. Another is dispensational: to look at different periods of time when God seems to be dealing with us in certain ways that differ from his dealings in others (for instance, Adam was not under the Mosaic Law. He didn't even *know* the Ten Commandments!).

Our main approach in this series is different. It is based on the *flow of history.* This is important for several reasons. First, God's revelation took place gradually. In the Old Testament period, revelation took place over many centuries of time; in the New Testament period, over decades. In each case there was a *progressive* dimension to revelation—truths were unfolded when needed by God's people, in a distinct sequence. We want to trace the unfolding of God's plan and purposes as it happens; we want to understand the Bible's teachings and events in their developmental sequence.

Second, God's revelation focused on contemporary needs. God spoke to living generations of believers, communicating the message they needed *then.* When we understand the crises that stimulated the communication of particular truths and the historical setting into which the revelation came, we have important insights into the meaning of the written Word for us in our day.

Third, the books of the Old and New Testaments do not appear in our Bibles in the sequence in which they were written. We need to place them in order if we want to see the process of history and fully understand God's Word.

For these major reasons, the overall approach in our **Bible Alive** survey studies is to explore God's Book in a sequence determined by Bible history. In *Springtime Coming,* we bring together in a unified whole the voices of the later Old Testament prophets.

TEACHING SURVEY

YOUR GOAL IN TEACHING Bible survey is to help your students master both the content of Scripture and its message. You want them to interact with the Bible, not just to read the textbook or listen to your lecture.

Teaching survey involves motivating your class to dig into the Word of God and then to explore together what the Bible says and what it means. How do the resources provided in the **Bible Alive Series** help?

The Bible. Most of your students' reading will be in the Bible itself. Help them select a good modern version, one that won't confuse or cloud the meaning by use of archaic English. Most quotations in this book are from the New American Standard Bible. Whatever text you choose, you will want to encourage your class members to use the same version—but invite them to check other translations and paraphrases when questions arise. Most of your class discussion will focus on the Bible text itself and on discoveries your students have made in reading the Word.

The textbooks. This book, and each of the **Bible Alive** texts, is designed to lead your students into the Bible. Each chapter organizes a distinct segment of Scripture (sometimes a chapter, sometimes several chapters or a book) in a way that will help your students fit that section together and also will sensitize them to its central message.

The texts, therefore, are not commentaries designed to "cover" the whole Bible or to tell the learner what he can discover in the Word for himself. Instead, each text is written to orient the learner to the Bible section being studied and to encourage him to move into the Word to make his own discoveries within the framework provided.

Often, when large sections of the Bible are being

discussed in a chapter, students will be asked to read only parts of that section in their Bibles. These parts are either *representative* passages (a sample of the larger segment) or *significant* passages (in which critical teaching or revelation is given). By using the textbooks to orient the reader to the scope and general impact of a section of Scripture, and then focusing attention for more intensive study of a representative or significant part of that section, maximum value for study time is assured.

Assignments. Each chapter in the text suggests two kinds of assignment. The first type involves reading and thinking, which *personalize* the message of Scripture. Such assignments are designed to help the learner meet God as He speaks to him through His Word today. Whether your students are members of a weekly Sunday School class or are in a course given for college or seminary credit, you will want to take time to talk over the *personalize* items.

Additional assignment suggestions are given with each chapter to help the student taking a credit course to *probe* beyond what might be expected of a less academic study. As the teacher, you may of course give any or all of these activities as assignments, or you may want to develop comparable assignments of your own. It is important, however, in the credit course as well as in the Sunday school or home Bible study class to make sure your students study the Scriptures for growth and enrichment, not just to attain information or pass examinations.

The class itself. Your time together in the class is important, particularly because, through discussion

USE OF RESOURCES

The Bible:
- the primary textbook; most time is to be spent in direct Bible study

The text:
- gives a framework for direct Bible study
- guides the student to explore representative or significant passages
- suggests assignments for personal Bible study

The class:
- helps students share discoveries
- allows learning activities to stimulate understanding and application of Bible portions read
- lets teacher add significant input, clarify, guide

Teacher supplement:
- suggests teaching goals for each session
- suggests teaching methods for each class session
- gives sample quizzes and exams

and various other teaching approaches, you can help your students think deeply about what they have studied in Scripture and its meaning for them today.

There is also a place, of course, for lecture and the input of your own ideas and research. The lesson plans suggest appropriate topics and resources for short lectures; you'll have material of your own you will feel is important as well. But in my own teaching of survey on a graduate level, I found that helping the truths of the Word come alive to my students was the most vital part of the course. The lesson plans include some of the methods I used then as well as the lectures, which are now, in large part, found in the chapters of the text.

TESTING AND GRADING

THERE IS GREAT VALUE in testing for both the leader and learner. The leader gains insight from good testing into the learner's growth in understanding and his response to truth. The learners gain confidence as they see evidence of growth. In fact, testing should be designed for just this kind of feedback. Good testing helps both leader and learner measure student growth.

Misuses of testing. Testing is all too often used for purposes other than providing feedback. Some leaders will design tests to reveal what the student does *not* know. Trick questions, or extremely difficult ones, can be used to construct those almost-impossible-to-pass exams that most of us have had to take at one time or another. Such tests help neither the leader nor the student.

At other times testing is viewed as a measurement approach through which grades will be assigned. When grading is based entirely on test performance, several negative elements are introduced into the learning situation. First, the test becomes a contest that forces good students to view others as rivals against whom they must compete. And that often leads poorer students to give up without trying. Thus the competitive dimension is unhealthy for both the good and the poorer student.

A second drawback to this kind of testing is that it places emphasis on verbal skills. One student may be able to work well with words and ideas and thus pass tests, while another who lacks the verbal facility may be touched far more and be more responsive in terms of changes in attitude and behavior. Too often our testing approaches reinforce the attitude that *knowing* rather than *doing* is important. Yet, the Bible teaches clearly that not just knowing but doing the Word is critical.

When we are teaching the Bible with a goal of spiritual growth, we want to make sure that the classroom atmosphere—*and testing*–encourage cooperation rather than competition. We want to help our students view each other as brothers and sisters who are ministering to one another. Competitive testing is definitely harmful to reaching such a goal.

And we want to be sure that our testing reinforces our stress on response to God's Word, not just the mastering of it as information.

To criticize testing as the basis of grading raises several questions. What *is* a valid basis for grading? How do we determine individual grades? What are grades supposed to represent anyway? Haven't grades in the past simply measured mastery of ideas, with personal growth seen as desirable but essentially ungradable?

Grading impact. Normally grading underlines

what is viewed as important by the teacher. When a teacher tests and grades only the mastery of cognitive material, then the students will tend to see only that as truly important. For this reason, in Bible teaching, grading *must* involve evaluation of the student's personal growth in responsiveness to God, at least to the extent that testing and other measurement methods go beyond mastery of mere information.

This suggestion is really not new or revolutionary. Many teachers include such factors as class participation and the consistent completion of daily assignments, reports, and written projects. What we are suggesting is simply that if grades are assigned, additional criteria and methods for grade determination also be used.

Grade criteria. What are valid criteria for the grading of Bible classes?

One approach, which permits use of many criteria and which also reduces the competitive and judgmental overtones of testing, is the contract method.

This involves announcing at the beginning of a course a basis on which students will be graded. When a course is taught for credit, the following requirements might be stated:

1. Everyone is expected to attend class and complete daily assignments.

2. Everyone is expected to take all quizzes and exams and to pass them with a minimum score of 75 percent. (Those who do not reach this minimum score will take the test over until they do.)

3. Students who successfully complete these first two requirements will receive a C grade. Students who wish to work for B or A grades can make a contract with the teacher. This contract specifies the extra work that they will do to earn the higher grade.

The advantages of this approach include setting and insisting on high standards of content mastery (75 percent to pass tests). It also includes great flexibility in letting students choose extra-credit projects on an individual interest basis.

For example, here are a number of contract possibilities for *Springtime Coming.* You may want to designate the ones you would accept—or suggest them, letting your students write their own contracts before consulting with you.

Of course, you will insist on a high quality of work being done in order for the contracted project to be acceptable.

SAMPLE CONTRACTS

1. Do at least one *probe* assignment in addition to the *personalize* assignments for each chapter.
2. Or do at least seven *probe* assignments in addition to the regular *personalize* assignments.
3. Or write a commentary on a selected prophetic section. Relate the material to the broad Old Testament prophetic picture, and show what that particular message meant to those to whom it was originally given. Explore several commentaries in developing your own.
4. Or, from the prophetic material studied, de-

velop a twenty- to twenty-five-page study of "The Role of Prophecy in Bringing Comfort and Hope to Israel." Or develop another statement of one of the functions of prophecy as you see it.

5. Or select one or two *values* that may be affected by prophetic material. Show how prophecy was designed to affect the selected value(s) when first given. Then show how our values today are affected by the prophetic vision. Use yourself as a "subject" in this paper; examine and share your own values and the impact of Scripture on them. The goal of this study is to help *you* grow spiritually; be honest with yourself as you write.

6. Or develop three sermons or lesson plans that seem to you to cover the heart of the Old Testament's prophetic message. Be concerned both with content and method: that is, how are you going to communicate with life-shaping impact the message you intend to get across?

These illustrations show some of the many kinds of contracts your students might undertake for special credit as you work together.

TEST MODELS

Our goal is to construct a test that will give feedback both to teacher and student on student growth. By *growth* I mean to indicate both learning (in the cognitive domain) and maturing (in the affective domain, where feelings, values, and attitudes as well as knowledge is important—and even in the area of choice and behavior).

Our testing task is made more challenging by realizing that within each domain are a number of levels, ranging from simple activities (such as recognizing true/false dichotomies or repeating a memorized word) to complex tasks (synthesizing, being able to apply principles, etc.). Here are a number of examples showing ways we might test on these various levels.

Cognitive domain. Mastery of content is an important element in all learning. Tests here range from ability to recognize, recall, and select from several possibilities to ability to relate, restate, integrate, and apply, etc.

Let's look first at several test models for measuring knowledge of content:

- True/False

______ *1. Daniel was a contemporary of Jeremiah.*

______ *2. King Xerxes is associated with the prophet Malachi.*

- Completion

1. Ezekiel's prophecy concerning the dry bones can be found in chapter ________.

2. In the Minor Prophets, a portrait of ______ ________ is typically found at the ending of the writing.

- Recall

1. List the major themes of Old Testament prophecy.

2. List the post-exilic prophets in order of their writing (date, not sequence in the Scriptures).

- Multiple choice

1. Malachi's prophecy portrays Israel some years after Nehemiah's ministry as ________.

(a) insensitive and unaware of their sinful attitudes and behavior.
(b) consciously rebelling against the injuctions of the Law.
(c) carefully following the pattern reestablished by the Wall-Builder.
(d) none of the above.

• Matching

Draw lines between items that are most closely related.

Daniel	*rebuilding the Temple*
Zechariah	*the last portrait of Israel*
Haggai	*times of Gentile dominion*
Malachi	*hopeful picture of the future*

Each of the above approaches tests possession of information on a relatively simple level. When we move to the *use* of knowledge, we test on significantly higher levels. These higher levels call for powers of integration, synthesis, and analysis—all of which, of course, presuppose possession of information. Here are some examples of this kind of testing.

• Type out paragraphs from several prophetic books. Then give the following instructions.

Look over the above paragraphs. Then do the following:

1. Identify the book from which each paragraph is taken, and explain your reasons for this identification.

2. Relate each paragraph to the portrait of the future sketched in the Old Testament.

3. Indicate what major prophetic themes should be added to give a more complete picture of the future, and state specifically where you would look in the Old Testament for this data.

• *Look at the following statement. Determine whether you agree or disagree with it. Then write a thorough defense of your point of view. The statement: "The primary value in a study of prophecy is found in discovery of the specific plan God has for the future and the ability knowledge of that plan gives us to evaluate the meaning of current events."*

• Open Bible:

Outline the book of Zechariah. Then from your outline demonstrate both the contributions and limitations of the Old Testament prophetic picture of the future.

Affective domain. The book *Taxonomy of Education Objectives: Handbook II: Affective Domain* by D. R. Krathwhol, et al (David McKay) gives many models for constructing test questions to measure attitudes, responses, and behaviors. Here are a few of them, adapted to this study of Old Testament prophecy.

• Response willingness

Have students circle A if they *do* the following, D if they rarely or never do it. Then circle for each item a W if the activity is engaged in willingly, a U if done unwillingly.

A D I completed personalize *projects as assigned. W U*
A D I read more than the assigned Bible passages. W U
A D I thought often about truths discovered. W U
A D I found my values and attitudes changing. W U

• Self-reporting helps us get at many kinds of affective data and lets the student become aware of his own personal growth. For example:

1. Select an Old Testament passage we studied that was particularly meaningful to you. Write a brief discussion of the section, and tell how studying it has affected your life.

2. *List as many values of the study of Old Testament prophecy as possible. Then write on* one *of these, explaining why this value is important to you.*

3. *Imagine that you lived in Daniel's time, either as a pagan who knew him or as one of the captive Israelites. Delineate how his life might have affected you. From your exposition, develop principles for believers today who wish to influence non-Christian friends or other Christians.*

4. *Imagine a friend who comes to you for counseling. You quickly see that the message of the Book of Esther may be just what she needs for comfort and encouragement. (a) Describe her problem. (b) Explain how Esther's message applies. (c) Share at least one way in which the message of Esther has been applied in your own life.*

• Another good way to give feedback to students is to use group process. Have teams of five (preferably who know one another) work on one of the following kinds of projects.

1. Let your students construct test questions (after giving them models to work from).

2. Let your students answer questions you construct as a group rather than individually.

3. Define growth goals that might reasonably be set for teaching this course in a local church setting. Then evaluate how (a) we might encourage reaching the goals and (b) how well the goals were reached in our own lives through this study.

In a very real way, the only test of success in Bible teaching is the learner's response to God's Word. Often this can be measured only after he has left the class. Bible survey is designed to motivate further

Bible study. If in later years our students become true explorers of the riches of God's Word, we have succeeded. The ability to pass an examination is evidence neither of your success as a teacher or the student's success as a student of God's Word. For this reason, the quizzes and tests are designed to give positive evidence of significant learning, to motivate and to encourage the student, and to help him focus on the important material.

However, testing is not always appropriate in a Sunday school or home Bible class situation, so your own particular setting for these **Bible Alive** studies must be evaluated carefully. Testing is least successful in classes where there is low commitment and/or high turnover. So, while it is recommended in general, there may be instances where it will hinder rather than help class attitudes.

Overall, test construction is an exciting and valuable part of effective teaching. Good tests will not only provide the teacher with information on student growth; they will also give the student a sense of accomplishment, which is vital to continued learning.

1

Ezra 1–6; Haggai

LOOK HOMEWARD

THE PROPHETIC MESSAGE assures us that God has a plan for this world and His people. Looking ahead and understanding His purposes, we have a unique hope. This first session is designed to focus your students' thoughts on the impact of hope.

It is important to set the tone of the classroom. If you are continuing from a previous **Bible Alive** study with the same group, your students already understand the relaxed discussion approach. If you have a new group, it is important to help them discover that their thoughts, feelings, and opinions are important here and that they will be encouraged to participate.

If your class is a continuation from an earlier study, you will already have distributed textbooks. Your students will have studied chapter 1 and the Bible passages. If this is a new class, your students will not have their texts or have studied in preparation for this class. Teaching ideas below are designed to fit either situation. Those teaching ideas marked by an asterisk (*) are to use in the new class situation.

Of course, you are free to adapt and supplement this lesson plan with your own ideas. The teaching hints are merely a guide and are not intended to limit your creativity in any way.

One reminder, however: You want to motivate your students to study the Bible text before class and to share with each other the meaning of God's Word as He speaks through it to them. So you will need to encourage *extensive class participation.* Because the students prepare for the classes, your role is not primarily to provide content. Content mastery is gained by direct Bible study before class.

LAUNCHING

These ideas are designed to encourage sharing and to motivate your students for the introduction to prophecy that will follow.

*1. Seat your students in a circle. Ask each student to share one thing he or she is really looking forward to. This may be something like a vacation, a visit from a loved one, retirement, whatever. After going around the circle once, go around again and ask each how the hope he or she has just shared affects his life. For instance, someone looking forward to a vacation may be reading travel brochures or folders about it, etc.

2. Seat your class in a circle. Ask each person to share one Bible prophecy he knows. List these Bible

prophecies on the chalkboard. When each person has had a chance to contribute, go around the circle again and ask each person to say how he feels the prophecy he mentioned might affect the daily life of a believer.

Take plenty of time for the launching. These sharing approaches are ways to let your students know that they'll contribute in your class and that you really are interested in their thoughts and ideas.

INPUT

Approach to the content of this lesson will vary critically, depending upon whether or not the students have prepared. For this reason, a number of suggestions are given from which you may choose.

*1. Place this period of Bible history in perspective. In a lecture, briefly review the Old Testament events that led up to the Exile. Use *Input* idea 2 to help your students sense the impact upon the people of Israel of being torn from the land.

*2. Before class, record on a cassette two persons, one man and one woman, reading the excerpts from Lamentations found on pages 11 and 12 of the textbook. Before you play the tape, ask your class to listen carefully for the *feelings* expressed. After your class reports their perceptions of their feelings, tell about the conditions of the exiles in Babylon, and show how their deep sense of loss was related to the sudden realization that God had deserted them.

*3. Another approach, after the *Launching* activity, is to give out the student textbooks. Ask each student to read quickly through the first chapter and to make a check mark beside each discovery that seems significant to him. When all have finished the rapid reading, let each person decide what in the chapter is most significant to him.

You can conclude the class by having your students share their perceptions, followed perhaps by a five- or six-minute closing lecture orienting them to the goal of this class (see below).

4. For those who've previously read the material, list on the board Israel's critical *change of direction* as reported in this chapter. You would include: taken into exile, prosperity in Babylon, Cyrus' appearance, return to Palestine, Temple foundations completed, oppositions, Temple work halted, sixteen years of struggle, Haggai's preaching, and Temple completion. These items should be placed in a column on the left side of the chalkboard. Then ask your students to talk through how each of these events might have affected the attitudes, motives, and confidence of the people of Israel. When the chart has been completed, ask your students: "Do you see any relationship between Israel's attitudes and the loss or reappearance of hope for their future?"

5. Another option is to tape-record the four sermons of Haggai (see chart on page 21). After hearing each message, ask your students what they heard as the basic appeal or thrust of the prophet's message. Talk these over, then focus on the fourth message as discussed in the textbook.

IMPACT

Each week in class you want to explore with your students the passages' meaning for today. In Bible teaching we are never satisfied with the mere coverage of content; we always want to go beyond to an exploration of truth's meaning. Each week's *Impact* ideas help you plan this important process.

*1. Conclude with a brief survey of the content of the textbook. Give each student this text, and show him how to use it. Students are first to read each chapter as an orientation and then study the Bible passages indicated, guided by the *Going Deeper* questions at the end of each chapter.

Then turn to the table of contents, and point out that in this particular course you will be looking together at the picture of the future given by God in the Old Testament. Just as looking forward to a future vacation has an impact on our actions now, many dimensions of the Christian's present life are guided by the prospects of Christ's coming and the events associated with it. When we understand what God intends for the future, we find a hope that gives us stability in spite of changing circumstances.

2. Organize your students in twosomes. Have each pair describe an individual who needs to hear the message of prophecy. Encourage your students to base their descriptions on the impact a prophesied event might be expected to have on attitudes, values, or behavior of the person who discovers and believes it.

After three to five minutes, call the group together and have each pair share their descriptions.

Close in prayer, confessing that you and each person in the class have a need to better understand our Christian hope and to live in the light of God's future.

ASSIGNMENT: Read text chapter 2, and do selected *Going Deeper* assignments on pages 23-24.

2

Historical Survey; Book of Esther

FROM THE ASHES

IN THIS SESSION you will deepen your students' awareness that the "unseen things," as Scripture puts it, are far more real and valuable than the visible. This conviction is extremely important when we deal with prophecy. The prophetic Word continually calls us to look beyond our present situation and to place our confidence in promises God has given us but have not yet been realized.

It is also one of your goals in this session, particularly if you are teaching this course for credit, to make sure that your students are familiar with the personalities and sequence of events covered in this period of Bible history.

LAUNCHING

Select one or more of the following.

1. If you are giving your class for credit, you might begin with a quiz. Before class, duplicate the chart

on page 34, leaving out significant events and persons. For example, you might omit "Temple foundation laid," "Daniel," "Ezekiel," etc., and perhaps one or two dates as well. But list the events, persons, and dates deleted below. Students should be able to fill in each listed item in the appropriate place.

Correct this quiz *in* class by having each student compare his chart with the one in the book. Stress the importance of knowing events and relationships for this period of Bible history.

2. To help your students see the importance of intangibles, and also to help them to continue to develop relationships with one another, divide them into groups of five. Each person is to introduce himself to the others as a person *without* any reference to his job, education, or role in his church, community, or family. Give about ten minutes for this activity.

Point out that most human beings seek their identity in their roles in society. Yet no one person can be summed up as "bank president" or "teacher." These roles do not really explain him.

3. Discuss briefly: Where did Israel look for her identity? What happened when Israel tried to find identity and meaning in material possessions and luxury? Where was Israel's real identity really rooted? (See pages 26-27 of the text.)

INPUT

Select one or more of the following.

1. It is appropriate to lecture on the impact of the

Captivity of Israel, briefly summarized in the text. Many other resources give further details. If you choose this option, be sure to point out that God's purposes were being fulfilled through historic events that on the surface appear to be disastrous to His plans and His people.

2. Your students have been asked to read Esther twice as an assignment. This fascinating book beautifully illustrates the reality and the importance of the unseen. For review of the story, have your students reconstruct the sequence of action recorded in the book. When you have the key events in the correct order on the chalkboard (using a *horizontal* time line), draw a large box around it. Now have your students add to the chart *what they believe to be God's actions or interventions behind the scenes.* Point out the fact that the unseen truly does have a fantastic impact on history and our lives. We can look to God and His forecast of events as trustworthy, for we experience His supernatural intervention daily.

IMPACT

Select one or more of the following.

1. Even if you use most of your time studying the history of the period, do use this *Impact* time to let your students share what they found to be the message of Esther to them.

You may do this by putting several summary sentences on the board. For example:

God does care for His own people.

God is with us even when we are not aware of Him.

God thwarts the plans of evil men.

Ask your class whether any one sums up the main "message to me" of the Book of Esther. Students can change the sentences, or can add sentences of their own, until each is satisfied.

2. If you do the Esther study above, move your class into a circle again. Give each person an opportunity to share one time when he or she now realizes God was acting in his life. Normally we do not see God's hand in events as we experience them. But looking back, how clearly God's loving supervision appears!

3. Conclude class by pointing out that in this study of prophecy many striking and amazing prospects for the future will be described. We dare never fall into the pattern of considering only tangible things as real. God's Word holds out an unseen hope; yet the most important things in our lives are unseen.

ASSIGNMENT: Read the text chapter 3 and do selected *Going Deeper* items.

3

Ezra 7–10; Book of Nehemiah

NEW BEGINNINGS

THESE TWO BOOKS PORTRAY the up and down experiences of Israel after the return from captivity. Their lives were marked by a series of turnings away from God's ordained life-style and a series of dramatic restorations, stimulated by key leaders.

This particular section of Scripture is a source of many insights. The lesson plan this week is developed to emphasize one theme: God's provision for restoration of wanderers. Your goal is to help your students overcome any sense of personal hopelessness and to explore God's eagerness to welcome them, should they need to return to Him now or at any future time.

LAUNCHING

Select one or more of the following.

1. Place on the board two sentences:

The believer should never need a fresh start in his relationship with God.

Every believer at times does need a fresh start in his relationship with God.

Ask your class to discuss the differences. Particularly they should explore the different ways each statement would be perceived if addressed to a person concerned about his own fellowship with the Lord.

2. Begin class by summarizing the experiences that demonstrated need for a return to God. These might include things such as the Levites leaving the Temple service for lack of tithes, the marriages with the pagan peoples, and other items revealed in both Ezra and Nehemiah. The failure to finish the Temple in Ezra's day, and to wall up the city in Nehemiah's, illustrate the discouraged state of Israel.

3. Following your outline of conditions, ask your class to brainstorm together indications in a Christian's life (or in a local congregation's life) that a fresh start is needed. Have your students try for at least twenty different indicators, and list their suggestions on the chalkboard.

4. Or ask your class to suggest ways the books of Ezra and Nehemiah might be applied by Christians today. This also could be a brainstorming activity. Some likely responses: Nehemiah might be used as a study for Christian leaders and leadership principles. Nehemiah and Ezra might be studied as a guide to prayer. Be sure that "how to make a fresh start" is on the list. After the list is placed on the board, discuss briefly which of these areas seem significant for most Christians.

If you want, divide into small groups to discuss application areas just listed. Let the groups use all but the last ten minutes of class time for discussion. The last ten minutes can be spent in reports.

INPUT

Select one or more of the following.

1. Have your students open their Bibles to the prayers of Ezra and Nehemiah (Ezra 9: 5-15; Neh. 1:4-11). Ask your students to explore these two. What common elements do they find? What principles are there for today? Do any prayer patterns emerge?

You might also explore with your class whether they believe these prayers are patterns for *every* time a believer comes to God, or only for special occasions or need. At what times would prayers like these be particularly appropriate?

2. Together study Nehemiah 10 in class. Focus particularly on verses 28-39, the covenant of the fresh start. What specifically is included in the covenant? How did these items relate to Israel's recent experience? What is done with the covenant? Why do you think a covenant is made?

Be sure to encourage discussion of the value of a covenant made by believers with God. What might such a covenant mean? What might it *not* mean? What might motivate us to make such a covenant?

3. After one or both of the studies above, discuss with your students their responses to *personalize* item 4, on page 46.

IMPACT

Select one or more of the following.

1. You might encourage your students to take five or ten minutes to individually write a personal covenant, patterned after the one in Nehemiah.

Or, you might discuss together a covenant statement that might be made by your local congregation.

2. Discuss Nehemiah 13. Point out that when Nehemiah left Jerusalem, the people fell into the old pattern of sin and failure. What was the quality that set Nehemiah apart and protected Israel when he was present? You might want to conclude with a brief exhortation to Nehemiah's kind of boldness, which in essence was simply faith to count on God and act boldly on what he knew was right. With this kind of boldness, we can avoid the up and down experience that characterizes too many believers.

ASSIGNMENT: Read text chapter 4; do selected *Going Deeper* items.

4

Book of Malachi

JOURNEY DOWNWARD

THIS SESSION SHOULD INCLUDE a survey of Malachi, a review of past history, and a launch into the study of prophecy that immediately follows.

LAUNCHING

Duplicate the Malachi study chart (page 57) on the board. When your students come in, work with them to fill in the chart, synthesizing their insights.

INPUT

1. Use the chart of the period from chapter 2. Review the exilic and post-exilic periods.

2. When the review is complete, ask your students to distinguish the times of "winter" and to explain why winter came at each of these points.

3. Look together at Malachi 3:16—4:5. Discuss how God seems to use these pictures of destiny com-

ing (see *personalize* item 2, page 57). As a class review, list "values for the believer" of a clear and vivid impression of the future.

4. Point out again the fact that the Christian is committed to the position that unseen things are more real and important than the things that can be seen. Prophecy, which gives the direction of history ahead, is extremely significant in keeping us from focusing our lives on the present alone. It is a corrective to materialistic and other concerns that constantly press upon us.

ASSIGNMENT: Text chapter 5; selected *Going Deeper* items. If you choose to have one of your students do the report on Daniel suggested in the next lesson plan, ask him to prepare.

5

Daniel 1–7

VISIONS IN THE NIGHT

YOU'LL WANT TO ACCOMPLISH two things in this class. First, you'll want to familiarize your students with Daniel's time and with Daniel as a person. You may choose to focus entirely on this for this lesson as you apply the many lessons we learn from his life to modern experience.

A second thrust, however, is to open the door to our study on prophecy. You may choose to develop this feature rather than the first. If you do, select those lesson activities that are related to Daniel's prophecy.

LAUNCHING

Select one or more of the following.

1. Have a student (who has previously been assigned this task) give a report on the times of Daniel. He should include the nature and glory of the Babylonian Empire, its extent, and something about the role Daniel played in that society. It might also be helpful if he correlated Nebuchadnezzar's time with events in other parts of the world such as Egypt, China, South America, etc.

2. How much should a Christian be involved in political life or seeking to influence the course of his own secular society? If this issue is of significance to your class, why not plan a brief debate with four speakers. Two each can challenge or defend the proposition that "Christians should not actively seek to influence the course of human society and government."

If you choose this option, do not spend more than fifteen minutes in debate. And select your debaters well ahead of time to give them opportunity to prepare.

3. If you wish to focus simply upon the person and character of Daniel, ask your students to each select one object in the room or on his or her person that seems in some way to express Daniel's character. Have each explain the object he chose.

INPUT

Select one or more of the following.

1. If you intend to focus this study as a preparation for prophecy study, give a lecture on miracles. There are several ways to develop this theme. You might survey the four periods mentioned in the text in which miracles came in clusters. Or you might discuss the question of miracles themselves. An excellent treatment of the question is found in a little paperback by C. S. Lewis, *Miracles*.

2. You may want to emphasize the relationship between Daniel and Nebuchadnezzar. Working from the Bible text, have your class work out a list of

incidents that portray that relationship. Put the list on the chalkboard. Discuss each incident briefly. Then, following through on *personalize* 2 on page 70, see if your class can come up with five values that were central in Daniel's life.

From them, can your class draw principles that might guide believers today to influence persons who are of higher rank or status than they? Influence might be exerted between an employee and employer or a student and teacher as well as within the family or within the local congregation.

IMPACT

Select one of the following:

1. If you focus on preparation for the prophecy, have your class turn together to Daniel 7. Talk at length about the difficulties they find in interpreting this prophecy accurately. What help might they need for accurate interpretation? What guidelines might be helpful?
2. Discuss briefly how Daniel personally was affected by his awareness of the unseen and by his vision for the future. It is not by chance that Daniel's godliness and his ministry as a chosen channel for Bible prophecy are linked. You might want to discuss 2 Peter 3 at this point and show the impact that awareness of the future is expected to have on the believer.

ASSIGNMENT: Text chapter 6; selected *Going Deeper* items.

6

Daniel 7–8

"I DECLARE NEW THINGS"

IN THIS CLASS SESSION you will familiarize your students with some of the principles (and problems!) of interpreting prophecy. We can be confident of the broad outline of the future sketched in Scripture. Many themes and events are clearly portrayed. At the same time, we want to help our students avoid the presumptuous certainty about details that all too often characterizes prophecy books.

This class should be very much a working session. It is almost entirely an *Input*-focused class.

LAUNCHING

Select one or more of the following.

1. Raise a simple question for a few moments of discussion—something like, "Why do you think astrology has such a hold on people today?" Or, "Do you know anyone involved in the occult? What do you think their motives or feelings are?"

After briefly discussing these questions, look together at the Isaiah quote found on page 73. Discuss, "What does this passage of Scripture say to the person involved in the occult? How might it make them feel? Why?"

2. You may want to move directly to lesson input. If so, a good way to start class is to put on the chalkboard an outline of the topics to be covered. Use the following outline or one of your own.

CLASS TODAY

I. Prophetic roots: Deuteronomy 19
II. Case study: Daniel 7–8
III. Interpretation
A. Principles
B. Problems

INPUT

Following through on the above outline:

1. Look with your class at Deuteronomy 19, pointing out why prophecy is given, who prophecy is given through, how the prophet is credentialed, and what prophecy is essentially concerned with. You'll want to note here that while a prophet often points out sins or faults in his contemporary society, his evaluations are rooted in earlier revelation. As we look at the predictive dimension of prophecy, it is not the daily life that is brought into focus but rather the future that looms immediately ahead or more distantly.

2. Trace through Daniel 7 and 8 carefully, relat-

ing the events described to subsequent history. To prepare for this, explore these passages more thoroughly in commentaries. They will give you further illustrations of the amazing accuracy of the prophetic picture. It is striking to note that while many of these predictions could not have been understood before the event, each word and phrase does reflect something fulfilled in the most literal way.

3. Then, using the textbook, work through the general principles and particularly the problems associated with prophetic interpretation. The problems outlined on pages 84-86 should not make us question the trustworthiness of the prophetic word. But they should make us hesitate to be too dogmatic in our interpretations.

IMPACT

If there is time left, you may wish to work through the Zechariah 9 passage together, as suggested in *personalize* 3. Rather than discuss it yourself, let your students share what they see in the passage as they apply some of the principles you've just discussed.

ASSIGNMENT: Text chapter 7; selected *Going Deeper* items.

In the student text on pages 94-96 of chapter seven, the author discusses two basic approaches to the understanding of prophecy: the literal-historical view and the spiritual-symbolic view. If we take the first, the result is a premillennial view of the future that sees a returning Jesus ruling an end time Kingdom here on earth. If we take the second, the result is an end time shrouded in mystery; prophetic Scriptures are interpreted figuratively to apply to Christians' present experiences.

At this point in the course, one of the two basic views must be taken. We're dealing now with extended Old Testament passages that must be understood from one standpoint or the other.

The author has chosen the literal-historical standpoint, with its resulting millennial position. If you wish, you can of course approach the same passages from the other standpoint—a choice of your own, even as the present text reflects the author's choice.

Resources that may help you develop lessons from that position include:

The Meaning of the Millennium, edited by Robert G. Clouse (InterVarsity, 1977).

The writings of George Eldon Ladd, such as *The Blessed Hope* (Eerdmans, 1956), *Crucial Questions About the Kingdom of God* (Eerdmans, 1952), and more recently, *The Presence of the Future: The Eschatology of Biblical Realism* (Eerdmans, 1973).

Finally, *The Prophecy of Daniel* by Edward J. Young (Eerdmans, 1949).

7

Daniel 9–12

THE COMING PRINCE

IN THIS AND THE FOLLOWING sessions, the emphasis will necessarily be upon mastery of content. This means that normally your *Input* section will be longer.

This week there are two thrusts: to communicate an appreciation for the accuracy and trustworthiness of Bible prophecy, and to begin developing an outline of prophesied events. You may, if you wish, spend the entire class on the first of these thrusts, as the other will be developed in subsequent lessons.

This is an area in which you'll want to do some personal research. Several books cited in the text will provide background data you can use in developing more information to present.

LAUNCHING

Select one or both of the following:

1. Begin class by placing the following chart on the

chalkboard. Ask several members of your class to "prophesy" something on the national or international scene that will happen within the next year. Then, ask others of the class to "prophesy" some things that will happen within the next five years. Finally, ask the rest of the class members to join in with "prophecies" about something within the next 100 years.

1 year	5 years	100 years

With these prophecies on the board, discuss together the likelihood of any or all of these happening.

2. If you think it would be helpful to your class at this point, you may wish to discuss together the question about modern-day "prophets" raised in *personalize* 3 on page 99.

INPUT

Select one or both of the following:

1. Cover the prophecy of the Coming Prince to be sure that each of your students understands it, its background, and its amazing partial fulfillment in the first coming of Christ (see pages 90-93).

2. Utilize the chart on page 92 to show the general

framework of this prophesied future. Then, in class, compare your students' answers to the questions raised under *personalize* 1 on page 99. Do not strive for detailed accuracy, and avoid disputes over details at this point. Remind your students that, as the last chapter pointed out, many aspects of prophecy caution us against being dogmatic in our interpretations.

IMPACT

You might discuss briefly the use of prophecy in apologetics and evangelism. Or if one of your students has undertaken a *probe* study in this area, invite him or her to give a brief report.

ASSIGNMENT: Text chapter 8; selected *Going Deeper* items.

8

Books of Zechariah and Zephaniah

WORDS OF HOPE

THIS SESSION AGAIN emphasizes content. In it you will begin to build the biblical portrait of the future, which will be discovered in these next weeks of study together. You will also give a brief orientation to the forms Old Testament prophecy takes.

LAUNCHING

Select one or both of the following:

1. When your students come in, ask them to pair off and to share with each other the "most interesting thing I discovered in studying this week."
2. If you wish, spend a few minutes letting the participants share what they and their partners talked about.

INPUT

You will probably want to cover each of these three areas this week.

1. Before you begin, outline the following topics on the chalkboard:

- Dress rehearsal principle
- Forms of prophecy
- Structure of prophetic books

Pages 101-3 point out that the themes of prophecy focusing on the end time have in fact been worked out over and over again in history. Discuss this point, and make sure that your students recognize the fact that while this repetition at times confuses us, Bible prophecy still does focus upon the culminating final period of history.

2. Take time in class to go through the four Zechariah passages that illustrate different forms of prophecy. This is discussed on pages 103 through 107 of the text.

3. Work with your class on the structure of prophetic books, as illustrated in Zephaniah. If you wish, scramble the outline of Zephaniah and place the pieces on the chalkboard. Then let your students work in groups of two or three to unscramble the outline and to find an illustration of each element in a specific verse of the Book of Zephaniah.

IMPACT

If there is time left over, discuss the chart on page 111 of the text. You'll want to give plenty of time for question-and-answer discussion. Also make sure that your class members realize again the lack of certainty concerning details of sequencing and timing.

ASSIGNMENT: Text chapter 9; selected *Going Deeper* items. Assign a student report on the history of Israel since 1948.

9

Deuteronomy 28–30; selected prophets

A FINAL REGATHERING

THIS CHAPTER INTRODUCES the first of the five major themes of Old Testament end time prophecy. A judgment-linked dispersal, followed by regathering, is a recurrent theme in both the prophets and Israel's history.

This session should be particularly interesting to your class because of its relationship to the current history of the nation Israel. Do some background study of the history of the Jewish state since 1948, or else assign this research to one of your students.

LAUNCHING

Select one or more of the following:

1. Begin with a brief sketch of the history of the Jewish state since 1948. You may give the report yourself, or ask one of your students to prepare it. Do not take more than five or ten minutes for the

report. But try to share some of the excitement and strain that has been associated with the short history of modern Israel.

2. You may find it helpful here to review the Law Covenant, particularly its existential nature. This is sketched in the text and stands alone of all the biblical covenants as focused on the present experience of God's people rather than upon the end time. For further information on the distinctiveness of this Covenant, see the second book in the **Bible Alive Series,** *Freedom Road.*

INPUT

Select one or both of the following:

1. Encourage your class to share insights they gained as they studied Deuteronomy 28—30. Make a list on the chalkboard of your students' observations about the pattern of foretold scattering and return.

2. Item 2 under *personalize* on page 127 lists a number of Bible passages dealing with this common Old Testament theme. Have each of your students look up one of these passages and be ready to read it aloud to the class. As each passage is read, encourage comments from your students, and make comments yourself on the insights gained.

As you work with these passages, remind your class of the distinction made in this chapter between the "often" and the "final" returns. See if you can determine which kind of return is in view for each and how to tell the difference.

IMPACT

Conclude with a reading and discussion of Ezekiel 37. What do your class members think? Could this describe the history of Israel since 1948? Is this return like or unlike the return described in Ezra and Nehemiah? How is Israel's present experience like or unlike the final return Scripture seems to describe?

Conclude by noting that if we *are* seeing Ezekiel 37 being fulfilled in our day, certainly the final time and the return of Christ is extremely near. The hope should be more real and present to us than at any other time in history.

ASSIGNMENT: Text chapter 10; selected *Going Deeper* items.

10

selected prophets

GREAT TRIBULATION

IN THIS SESSION another end time theme of the Old Testament prophets is explored. Tribulation as a purposeful and purifying experience for God's people is covered in the chapter and will be the focus of your in-class study.

You may have a number of goals for this study. One is simply to understand something of the prophesied time under consideration. Another has to do with the relationship of Christ's Second Coming to the tribulation. A third relates to the role tribulation generally has in God's plan for His people. You are of course free to select the emphasis you feel is most appropriate for your own class.

If you are teaching this class for credit, or with primary concern for content mastery, you will want to encourage your students to begin preparing for a test now. One approach: give a five- or ten-question quiz to begin the class hour, using the kind of questions you intend to use in the final examination. (See the testing section of this guide for suggestions.)

LAUNCHING

Begin by giving your class a feel for the events and impact of the tribulation. Play a tape recording using several different voices who read with dramatic effect part or all of the verses listed under *personalize* 1 on pages 140-141.

INPUT

Select one or more of the following:

1. Debate the relationship of the Rapture of the Church to the tribulation. This issue has not been explored in depth in this chapter. Unless this is of particular interest to the class, it is probably wise not to spend too much time considering it.

You may wish to explore reasons for one position or the other in a brief lecture. Again, however, do not make this a primary focus of your class.

2. Explain the fact that Christ's comings (whether first or second) involve periods of time rather than being single, isolated events. In this chapter your students have been given a survey of a number of events students of prophecy believe are associated with the Second Coming.

To explore both the sequence and the events, work through Zechariah 10—14 with your class. This study was assigned in *personalize* 2. Locate the major events, and watch for hints concerning sequence. You will, of course, want to work through the Zechariah passage yourself ahead of time and come to class with an outline from which to organize the class discussion.

3. You may want to go back and to explore some of the Day of the Lord and tribulation passages from *personalize* 1. Your students can develop a sense of the character and the purpose of the tribulation.

IMPACT

Spend fifteen to twenty minutes of the class time helping to focus your students on their own attitude toward tribulation. Whether or not the believer goes through the great tribulation, each of us does experience trials which are purposeful. There are a number of ways you might lead into an exploration of this theme.

1. Even if direct interpretation of the Old Testament tribulation indicates it relates only to Israel, there may be application to the believer's present experience. Looking at the purposes expressed for Israel and the tribulation in the Old Testament, we can see purposes that God may have for our own difficult times. Use the questions under *personalize* 3 on page 141 to stimulate a discussion.

2. Habakkuk faced the same promise of impending tribulation. Chapter 3 of his book tells his reactions and particularly his fear (vv. 1-2), which becomes faith (vv. 17-19). How does this give us guidance for our own response to tribulation?

ASSIGNMENT: Text chapter 11; selected *Going Deeper* items. Assign reports to your class members for the characters in your next study. See next page for details.

11

selected prophets

THE CAST OF CHARACTERS

IN THIS SESSION you will familiarize your class members with end time events. You'll also work in detail on Ezekiel 38 and 39.

This is again an information-focused lesson. As a support tool, you may want a large map of Europe and the Near East.

LAUNCHING

Select one or more of the following:

1. Begin with reports from your students. Before class, ask selected students to prepare reports on the primary actors in the end time drama. This should include reports on each of the great world powers (the West, North, and possibly a combined report on the East and South). Several passages are suggested in the text as resources. You may want to suggest additional sources for research. The report should also include the Antichrist.

Or you may wish to summarize this material yourself in an introductory lecture.

It is very helpful to have a map here, so that each reporter can point out the world areas involved.

2. Or you might want to begin with a pantomime, acting out the end time events. This would involve choosing a person to represent each of the cast of characters. Action, if you choose this approach, would be as follows:

Seated in a chair is a person labeled *Israel.* To the north of seated Israel, have an individual standing labeled *Russia;* to the south, an individual labeled *Egypt;* to the west, an individual labeled *Western European.* Another individual labeled *Antichrist* will tie strings to West for manipulation.

As action begins, the North and South make threatening motions against Israel. The West, manipulated by Antichrist, holds up hands in warning and acts out the signing of a treaty with Israel.

At this point Israel, who has looked concerned, relaxes in the chair. West returns to its place.

South then hops up and begins to attack Israel. West steps in and with one blow drives Egypt out of the scene. West returns to place.

Russia then attacks Israel. The West, rather than intervening, watches. Russia throws Israel to the floor and stamps on the prostrate body. Standing victoriously, Russia is suddenly struck from offstage by divine intervention. Russia staggers back and collapses off the scene.

Whereupon the West moves to prostrate Israel and stands with its foot on Israel, taking a victorious position.

After acting out the skit, see if your class members can reconstruct what the action portrays.

INPUT

Select one or more of the following

1. Using a map, trace the action portrayed. Follow the general pattern outlined by Pentecost and reprinted in this chapter.

2. Divide your students into groups of three or four. Ask them to read the Ezekiel chapters carefully. Working together, they should develop a series of newspaper headlines showing how the events might be reported in a modern newspaper. If you wish, they may spend time developing the story a bit.

3. This would be a good opportunity for your students to work together in groups comparing the charts of the end times they have been working on in their own books. Move from group to group and answer questions that may arise.

Following the chart work, you may want to have the class come together for discussion.

IMPACT

Last week you discussed how the history of Israel from 1948 appears to set the scene for the end time, as portrayed in Scripture. This week it might be of interest to sketch the changing map of Europe over the same period of time. The partition of Germany, the rise of the Common Market, and the extension of Russian influence all seem particularly significant in view of the fact that they currently include just those territories that seem to be the subject of Bible prophecy. Also of significance is the increasing enmity of the Arab powers and the formation of an OPEC bloc of nations that corresponds significantly with the biblical portrait of the South.

These present political movements are not *proof* that the time of the end is drawing near. But they are certainly indicative that the situation sketched in the Old Testament could be duplicated, in specific detail, in a startlingly short time.

ASSIGNMENT: Text chapter 12; selected *Going Deeper* items.

12

selected prophets

THE GLORIOUS KINGDOM

THIS WEEK WE'RE MOVING beyond the tribulation period to look at another major theme of the Old Testament prophetic picture. We will see portraits of the glorious Kingdom, of the earth restored to Eden-like blessing. This week you'll want to spend time not only to sharpen your students' portrait of that Kingdom but also to help your class members to explore together the meaning of the picture.

If you are planning to give a test, you'll want to decide by this time whether to use a class hour or give a take-home examination. Check again the options discussed under testing on pages 192-201.

LAUNCHING

As your students come in, have a recording of the song "The King Is Coming" playing in the room. When all are present, sing the song together and then ask for personal responses. What is the most exciting thing to each about the coming of the King?

INPUT

This week follow the process suggested by the *Going Deeper* questions, found on pages 162-64. You might begin by dividing the class into two large groups. Pair off the students in each group. Have the pairs in the first group look up five Kingdom references (see *personalize* 1). Students in the other group will examine five references from the list on pages 159-60. After this review, let your students come together and share significant discoveries.

Move on then to do the activities and discuss the questions listed under *personalize* 3 and 4 on pages 162-63.

IMPACT

1. Read together 1 Corinthians 15:24-28. You might also include Romans 8:18-23.

Conclude by singing "The King Is Coming" once again.

ASSIGNMENT: Text chapter 13; selected *Going Deeper* items. You may also wish to ask each student to present five questions he thinks ought to be included on a final examination to indicate mastery of the Bible texts and/or mastery of their meaning.

13

selected New Testament passages

OLD TESTAMENT . . . OR NEW?

THIS LAST SESSION ATTEMPTS to summarize the thrust and impact of Bible prophecy. Particularly you will be concerned to demonstrate the relationship between the Old and New Testament prophetic pictures. As the text points out, the relationship is one of correspondence and harmony, highlighted by different emphases. The New Testament tends to emphasize the period beyond what is portrayed in the Old Testament. But, as the passages quoted in the chapter clearly indicate, there is complete harmony between both Testaments in their view of the future.

The lesson plan below suggests a variety of learning activities that you may want to build into the classroom process. Select from them to develop the thrust you feel most important for your class. But do be sure to spend plenty of time in sharing by the class what your prophetic studies have meant to them.

LAUNCHING

Select one or more of the following:

1. Go around the circle and ask your students to recall what impressions of the future they had before they began this springtime study. Have these impressions changed? If so, how?

2. Ask your students to write a sentence or two explaining their understanding of the relationship between Old and New Testament prophecies. Have several read their sentences and discuss briefly.

INPUT

Select one or more of the following:

1. Together work through Matthew 24—25. Note particularly the elements of correspondence with the Old Testament prophetic picture. Also note carefully chapter 25's exhortation to watchfulness. An understanding of the fast-approaching future is clearly designed to motivate the believer in his present experience.

For a detailed examination of these chapters, see chapter 11 in the first **Bible Alive** New Testament book, *The Servant King.*

2. In class, assign your students to read quickly either 1 or 2 Thessalonians. Each should mark an *X* by verses that are prophetic. Come together to hear reports. As each prophetic passage is pointed out by your students, look together at the text to see how it is applied by Paul to the life of the believers. Strikingly, prophecy is seen in these two books to have the greatest possible impact on daily life.

IMPACT

Select one or more of the following:

1. As you come to the end of the study, discuss values of the study of prophecy for the believer (see pages 173-74). Encourage your class to think of a variety of applications but also to share the personal impact the study has had on them.

2. Or discuss the questions raised under *personalize* 2. Be sure to focus on values, attitudes, and life-style changes your students may have experienced.

3. You might conclude class by reading together the Romans 11:33-36 doxology, affirming the greatness and complexity of God's wise plan.

5.37
4.45
92